THE WEB DESIGNER'S IDEA BOOK

volume 2

PATRICK McNEIL, creator of designmeltdown.com

THE WEB DESIGNER'S volume 2
IDEA BOOK

more of the best themes, trends and styles in website design

HOW
BOOKS
Cincinnati, Ohio
www.howdesign.com

For more excellent books and resources for designers, visit www.howdesign.com.

14 13 12 11   5 4 3 2

Distributed in Canada by Fraser Direct
100 Armstrong Avenue
Georgetown, Ontario, Canada L7G 5S4
Tel: (905) 877-4411

Distributed in the U.K and Europe by F+W Media International
Brunel House, Newton Abbot, Devon, TQ12 4PU, England
Tel: (+44) 1626-323200, Fax: (+44) 1626-323319
E-mail: postmaster@davidandcharles.co.uk

Distributed in Australia by Capricorn Link
P.O. Box 704, Windsor, NSW 2756 Australia
Tel: (02) 4577-3555

Cataloging-in-Publication data can be found on record at the Library of Congress.

Edited by Amy Schell Owen
Designed by Grace Ring
Production coordinated by Greg Nock

DEDICATION

For Angela and Jack.

ABOUT THE AUTHOR

Patrick McNeil is a web developer focused on content management systems and front-end web development. His love for both technology and design makes the web his ideal playground, and his diverse interests allow him to be involved in everything from writing and speaking at conferences to digging into jQuery and advanced content management system integrations. Ultimately, his love for design drives him to obsess over cataloging web sites into the various trends and patterns presented in this very book.

ACKNOWLEDGMENTS

As with the first *Web Designer's Idea Book,* I can't imagine how I could thank anyone for making this second volume without first acknowledging the countless designers who worked so hard to make the designs presented in this book. It is the work of others that inspires me to obsess over web design, and I truly appreciate the passion you pour into your work. I also owe many thanks to the readers and fans of Design Meltdown and the first book; your response far exceeded my expectations and I am grateful for your support. While many people at F+W Media make a book like this possible, I particularly appreciate Amy and Grace's efforts to help push this book to be the best it can be. And as always, my wife Angela is my biggest supporter: She encourages me to chase my dreams and sacrifices countless hours as I stay up late writing.

table of contents

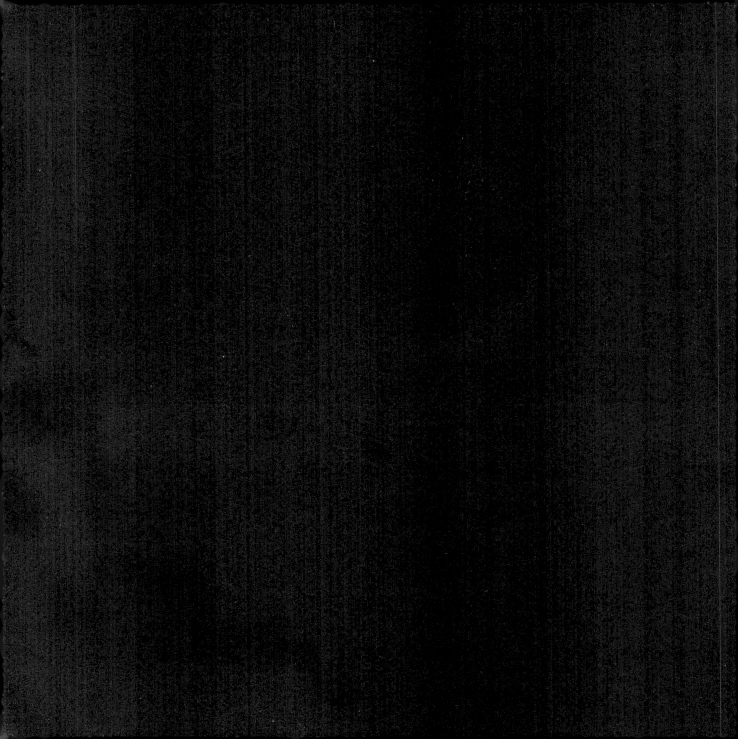

word from the author

The web is one of the fastest-changing mediums creatives can hope to work in. The styles come and go as quickly as you can imagine, and new development techniques are always emerging. These new techniques lead to other trends and patterns that turn up in countless web sites. On the whole, I am thrilled to see how the web industry is progressing. The past year was a good one for web design. We saw many of the web 2.0 fads fade, such as frivolous badges and an insatiable use of glossy designs; in their place, a refined style with a sense of purpose has emerged.

I can't help but reflect on how much things have changed since the original *Web Designer's Idea Book*, especially from a technology standpoint. With much wider acceptance of JavaScript-based tools than ever before, libraries like jQuery continue to shape the face of web sites. Flash, while still ever-present, has more and more found its place in the myriad of web development tools and is no longer the de facto standard for sites that demand to be amazing. And mobile platforms have become an unstoppable force that will drive change in the industry. The web is evolving, the same as it always has. If you're up for it, the web industry offers endless opportunities to grow and learn. And this is just what I and so many others are addicted to.

It is this addiction which drives me to obsess over trends and patterns and form them into this book. In fact, I am already thinking about what books three and four might contain. I believe I share this insatiable appetite for learning, growth and better understanding with many people in my field. There is a reason you can google almost any web development problem and quickly find an answer. We are a community of people passionate about what we do and fearless about sharing that knowledge. I sincerely hope that this book can be part of my contribution to the web community.

—Patrick McNeil

Note: If you would like to submit your designs for possible use in future books, please visit TheWebDesignersIdea Book.com to sign up for our semi-annual mailing list. You will be informed of book releases, calls for entries and other information directly related to the books. Submitting sites is free, easy to do and is open to anyone. And if you think you are too small of a shop to submit your work, I encourage you to do so anyway. I pride myself on profiling many lesser-known sites. My books showcase what is happening on the web, not just the most expensive sites.

01 /

inspiration

One of the questions I get asked most is how to leverage inspiration without plagiarizing or stealing someone else's ideas. In some ways, this is a really easy question, simply answered. Don't steal ideas. The nuance of this is the hard part. At what point does inspiration become theft? The lines are blurry, especially when we consider the fact that no one operates in a bubble. All design is influenced by the previously created works we are surrounded by. Marko Prljić is a web designer who has also written on this very topic. This chapter, penned by Marko, takes us step-by-step through the creation of a new design. More importantly, it demonstrates how various ideas, approaches and design elements can be found elsewhere and merged together to create a new design. I am excited for this book to inspire you and challenge you to borrow ideas—without ripping them off.

using inspiration in the design process

By Marko Prljić

Get inspired, but don't copy. There is a thin line between inspiration and copying—one that is further blurred as we are surrounded with designs and art in our everyday lives. Finding inspiration for a design is an easy task these days, having so many valuable resources to leverage. The web has been inundated with web design showcases. There is no exact formula for how to use inspiration and not copy someone else's work, but there are some straightforward ways to avoid it. Here, I will take you through my design process for a web site I recently created. Through examples of inspiration, I will demonstrate how I created a fresh and new design while leveraging various sources of inspiration. But before we step through an example, let's look at some core concepts when it comes to using inspiration.

USE MORE THAN ONE DESIGN FOR INSPIRATION

When you have found a design that you like and you think, "I could do something like this," don't stop there; keep searching for additional designs that are similar in color, structure or content to what you have in mind. The goal will be to leverage the best elements of each of these as you merge these ideas into your new layout.

Start visualizing your new design with a combination of elements that inspire you. Look at the wire frames for your new site, and consider styles that might be applied to specific elements. The goal is not to pick a single design and copy it, but rather to find an assortment of elements that can work together in a new way. By the time you start creating mock-ups, you should have developed some fresh ideas with the result being something new and—most critically—unique.

BREAK THE DESIGNS DOWN

A great way to approach inspiration is not to look at the whole design, but rather to scan for the elements that are relevant to your project. Observe how others have solved problems similar to yours, and run with those aspects of the design. For example, the following observations on imagery could be made from this sample site (Figure 1 on the next page):

- The header is not split off by contrasting colors or boxes like typical sites are.
- The color palette is limited with lots of subtle tones.
- A large tagline clearly states the site's purpose.
- The large slide show has a clear set of icons below it, giving a sense of placement in the show.

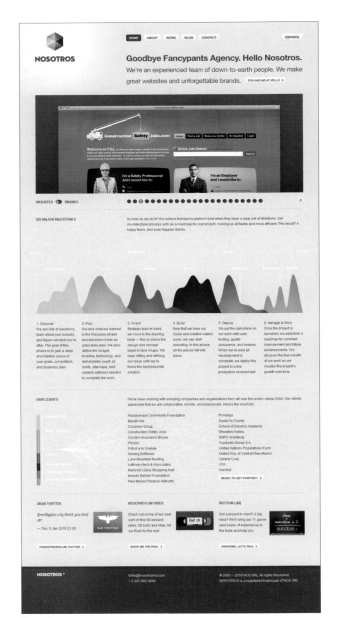

Figure 1

Figure 2

Figure 3

- Lots of white (or gray) space makes the site feel comfortable and open.

PICK YOUR FAVORITE DETAILS

When you have found some designs that inspire you, take a closer look and pick out the elements that really make them shine. Watch for gradients, light effects, typography—all of the subtle details that breathe life into the design. Ask yourself: What is it that makes this design so great? Figure 2 is another good example with some key elements highlighted.

THE CREATION OF A NEW DESIGN

Now let's dig into an example of this and step through the design process used for the creation of a template I designed for themeforest.net. Several great sites inspired this design, and I will demonstrate how they contributed to the final product. Let's start by taking a look at the final product in Figure 3.

When I started the design for this template, I thought about how it would be nice to create something modern, well-structured, content-rich, blog-adaptive and multifunctional. With this in mind, I had a vague idea of how the design should feel.

Figure 4 Inspiration

Figure 5 Design

Figure 6 Inspiration

Figure 7 Design

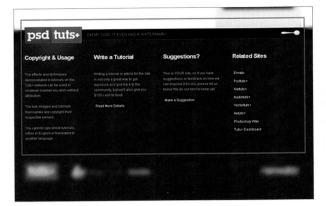

Figure 8 Inspiration

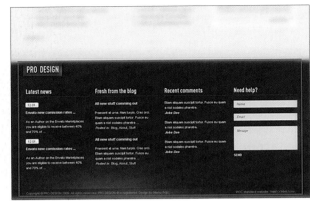

Figure 9 Design

From there, I found these organizations' sites as sources of inspiration:

- FreelanceSwitch
- Aviary
- Psdtuts+

Inspiration #1: FreelanceSwitch

The first thing I loved about this site's design was its navigation: It's big and clear, and contains small additional bits of information for each link. It also has multiple layers to the background, stretching from top to bottom, giving the site a more interesting look (Figures 4 and 5).

Inspiration #2: Aviary

The large content rotator on this homepage works great, so I thought this could be a key element of my design. This is a common design element, but it's great to see how others have approached it. There are a million ways to add variety to an element such as this through subtle changes in the configuration and layout (Figures 6 and 7).

Inspiration #3: PsdTuts+

A key element borrowed from this design is the footer. It's rather large, and it provides additional information and key links. I also noticed how the logo is repeated in the footer, so I tried the same thing with my own stylization (Figures 8 and 9).

CONCLUSION

If you look at the finished product, you can see how the various sources of inspiration contributed to it, and yet the result is a fresh design that doesn't feel like a direct replication of any of the other designs. Some will say I am suggesting you Frankenstein together various pieces to form a new design. Certainly, if you simply clip together various elements, the results are not likely to inspire anyone in a positive way. You must always work to unify the new work with common stylistic approaches and never lose track of the big picture. In the end, be inspired—but don't copy!

02/

basic principles
of design

My approach to design analysis and learning has always been from a sample standpoint. That is to say, I much prefer to analyze samples of design and how they address various issues, rather than talking abstractly about vague topics. Through the analysis of real-life examples, we get a practical overview on the basic underlying principles of design. This is good not only for the beginner, but also for the more advanced designer. I often find that when I go back to the basics, I find something new that gives me a fresh perspective. It also seems that whenever a design is suffering, I need only to review the list of basic principles to be reminded of an aspect of the design I have neglected.

For the basic principles covered here, I turned to the book *Basics of Design* by Lisa Graham. It is the book I used in school, and it has always served as a basic reference point for me. According to Lisa, all design is built on the basic principles of emphasis, contrast, balance, alignment, repetition and flow. The more thought that is put into these elements, the better the design is likely to be. When these principles are forgotten, a design often goes astray. By returning to the fundamentals, you can refocus your eyes and mind to produce an exceptional design.

However, keep in mind that simply following a formula doesn't guarantee success: I'm not saying that this is the formula to good design. I can say, though, that time and time again, these principles are what encourage me to polish my own designs and allow me to discover why some designs work and others fail.

In this section, a focused effort has been made to provide examples of sites that demonstrate these elements in a variety of ways. Some samples use them in strikingly obvious ways, while others are more subtle. This is what I love about real-life examples, though; they are much more practical for illustrating a point because nothing in the real world happens in textbook-perfect patterns.

emphasis

Emphasis highlights a special importance or significance, and in many ways emphasis is closely related to, if not the same as, hierarchy. In order to design around the principle of emphasis, you must analyze a site's content in order to determine what hierarchy of importance the content should use. Once this is established, you can create a design that effectively carries out the hierarchy. A great method to establish what needs emphasis is to list all of the elements required on a page. Then, number the elements in order of importance. With this list in mind, design so that the visual hierarchy of the page reflects the determined importance. One reason this is so important is to avoid an attempt to emphasize everything. It also helps avoid the trap of an accidental hierarchy. It is always better to consciously decide what should be the visual priority and not just leave it to chance. If you try to emphasize everything, you effectively emphasize nothing. Let's look at some samples to see what has been done to create a visual hierarchy.

Bryan Connor (Figure 1)

Bryan Connor's site is a great demonstration of emphasis. The most prominent element of the page is the most recent post from his blog. It has a sharp contrast to the majority of the page by being the only white section, and the type is large and placed near the top of the page. This is a sign of clear intention and a desire to direct attention. In cases like this, it might be tempting to think the portfolio pieces or the contact information should be equally important, but again, trying to make everything equal ultimately makes everything blend together.

Digitalmash (Figure 2)

This site offers another clear use of emphasis to control the user's consumption of the page. The large, dominant text, which has again been placed at the top of the page, clearly states the site owner's purpose: This site is intended to get him work. It's not there to show off to his family, to share Flickr photos with friends or to hype up his latest tweet. It's simply to drum up work. Consider your site's purpose and how you can use emphasis to bring it out and highlight it.

Cold Stone Creamery (Figure 3)

This site offers a common layout formula that leverages effective emphasis. The page has a typical header containing a logo and key navigation items. From there, the design starts with a very strong emphasis. Primarily controlled by the amount of physical space elements occupy, the emphasis of items is reduced as you move down the page. Some sites will have more than the three layers we find here, but that is not necessarily required.

Here, the large masthead movie directs the user's attention and offers the sites owners to direct user attention as they see fit. Then the design moves into a denser content region with three messages in separate buckets. This density means it will be looked at second and not first. It makes really good sense to match the flow of emphasis to the way a user engages a page: top to bottom. Don't fight it, just go with it and work it to your advantage.

Figure 1 http://www.bryanconnor.com

Figure 2 http://www.digitalmash.com

Figure 3 http://www.coldstonecreamery.com

http://www.greencircleshoppingcenter.com

http://www.serj.ca

http://www.smartosc.com

http://stonetire.com

http://www.atebits.com

contrast

Contrast is the visual differentiation of two or more elements. Elements with strong contrast appear distinct and separate, while elements with low contrast appear similar and tend to blend together. There are many design elements you can manipulate to achieve contrast, including color, size, position, font choice and font weights. Contrast in a design will help a site have visual variety and avoid being stale. Contrast can also help achieve focus, thereby addressing the need for emphasis on certain elements. You can see how a loop among the basic design principles appears, as contrast is used to affect emphasis, flow and other aspects of a design.

Contrast may have its largest impact on the hierarchy of a page, as it is often used to enforce the desired emphasis. In this way, contrast can contribute to the visual order of a design. It can quickly draw attention to key elements, such as content, action items or purpose statements. As always, the needs of a site should be carefully considered so you can intentionally draw attention to certain elements though the deliberate control of contrast. Let's look at some samples to see what other designers have done with contrast.

Twe4ked Studios (Figure 1)

In this example, it is easy to spot the contrast because the two large green buttons leap out of the page. These key calls to action have been emphasized through size and color. Clearly the designer of this site is driving at two purposes; he wants you to either look at his portfolio or give him a call. We also find contrast at work in a few other areas on this site. His introduction is large and dominates the top of the page. Not only is it the full width of the page, but it is also the largest text on it. The entire top half of the page is black on white with the bottom being reversed out. This contrast sets the top content apart with an apparent level of importance, which is further emphasized by the contrast in type density. The content in the bottom is far denser, making it feel less important. It's amazing how fundamental contrast is and how inescapable it can be.

Be the Middle Man (Figure 2)

This site again demonstrates how a radical use of contrast can drive emphasis and the desired action for your user. This site encourages the user to test out their search tool by making it a dominate element in the page. As such, their goal is clear. Another interesting aspect of this design is how the density of content gets greater as the page goes down. This increasing contrast flows nicely and matches a user's behavior. If a person is reading this page to the bottom, chances are he is more and more interested as he reaches the bottom of the page (or perhaps more desperate to find what he needs), so the site packs in more and more to try to offer up what the user is looking for.

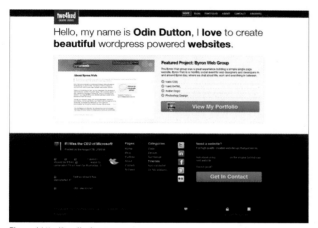

Figure 1 http://twe4ked.com

http://www.swgraphic.com/v2

Figure 2 http://www.bethemiddleman.com

http://www.onebyfourstudio.com

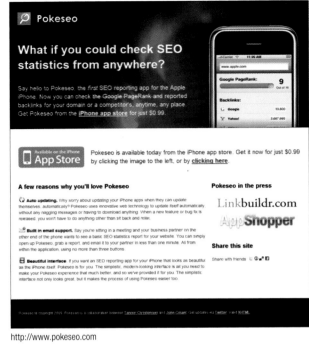

http://www.pokeseo.com

http://www.mediacontour.com

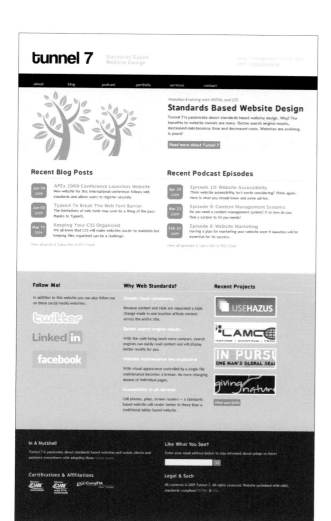

http://www.tunnel7.com

http://andrewlindstrom.com

http://www.allisclear.com

balance

The principle of balance revolves around the idea of how the elements in a design are distributed and how they relate to the overall distribution of visual weight within the page. This has a considerable impact on the visual stability of the design. As elements are grouped together in a design, they create visual weight. Typically, this weight must be balanced out by an equal and opposite weight in order to achieve balance in the design. Not doing so results in a design that feels unstable, though this is not to imply that it would be necessarily bad. I have no doubt that a lack of balance could be put to effective use. But a well-balanced design creates a subtle notion of stability and is generally more appealing.

There are two approaches to balance: symmetrical and asymmetrical. We will look at examples of each.

SYMMETRICAL BALANCE

Balance through symmetrical design is accomplished when the design of a page is mirrored on some axis and the two halves have identical visual weights. In web design, this is typically seen when the left and right sides are split vertically and each side has an equal weight. As always, I prefer samples, so let's look at one.

MINT Wheels (Figure 1)

The use of symmetrical balance matches with the content of this site in a very natural way. Consider the precise efforts that go into ensuring perfect balance in luxury cars; these cars offer up some of the most perfectly balanced experiences one can find on the road. In this way, a symmetrically balanced site fits well with the type of experience one has when driving a car such as this. Note how the logo has been moved to the top center of the page. This

not only helps establish symmetrical balance, but also puts the logo in the visual hot spot for the layout (top and center). This site is slick and clean, and it perfectly matches its content.

ASYMMETRICAL BALANCE

Asymmetrical balance is achieved when the visual weight of a page is equally distributed on an axis, but the individual elements of these halves are not mirror images. That is a really complex way of saying that asymmetrical balance is a result of the use of dissimilar elements to create an overall balance. That still sounds complicated; let's look at some samples to see how this works.

Dallas Baptist University (Figure 2)

Asymmetrical balance is extremely common in web design because it is often a more natural solution to the content being presented. In this case, we see asymmetrical balance throughout the page, starting with the header. The logo balances out the main navigation items (which have been placed where the logo usually resides). The logo is tall and dark, allowing its small size to still match up with the navigation. Bellow the banner section, the text box with the welcome message is larger than the denser quick facts section. The size of the left box is well matched by the smaller but denser box next to it.

Campaign Monitor (Figure 3)

In some cases, it will make most sense to actually blend these two approaches to achieving balance. This is exactly the approach taken on the Campaign Monitor landing page. At the top, we see asymmetrical balance with the copy section balancing the image. But below that, we see a section of balance where the six items, the logos below that and the footer copy are all perfectly balanced left to right in a symmetrical way.

Balance is one of the more subtle elements of design, and one that many of us will address instinctively. If your design feels lopsided, consider how you can balance it by minimizing the contrast. This might mean two dominant elements that match well, or a set of equally controlled, less prominent items to balance it out. Does your design feel like it would tip over? Does it feel unstable? These are the types of questions to ask yourself to discover if you have balance issues.

Figure 1 http://www.mintwheels.com

Figure 2 http://whydbu.dbu.edu

Figure 3 http://campaignmonitor.com/designers

http://viminteractive.com

http://www.nationalbreastcancer.org

http://bunton.com.au

http://www.mdswebstudios.com

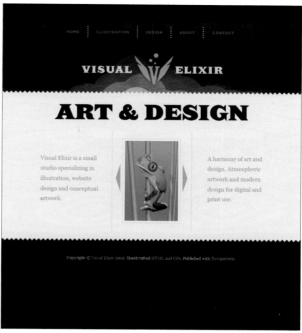

http://www.visualelixir.com

http://www.typejockeys.com

alignment

Alignment is the arrangement of elements in such a way that the natural lines (or borders) created by them match up as closely as possible. By doing so, these elements become unified and form a greater whole. This is often referred to as working with a grid. Unaligned elements tend to fall apart and lack the unification we so often seek. Some examples of aligned elements are having the tops of two columns line up, or the left edges of a series of stacked elements align with each other. While these examples are fairly obvious, there can be far more intricate alignments in a page that work to create a unified and pleasing design.

If you have been given the task of taking designs and turning them into code, you should be particularly aware of this principle. As a design is translated into reality, it often becomes tedious and difficult to replicate the alignments established in the original design. Not only is it a challenge, it also can be easy to overlook these carefully crafted details entirely. An awareness of design on this level can really help a developer in the translation process.

Design Without Frontiers (Figure 1)

This site is like the poster child for demonstrating alignment in web design. The deliberate and consistent use of alignment makes for a design that feels clean and balanced. For example the width of the logo matches the width of the content and the titles all align. Thanks to the nature of this design, one need only follow the lines to see what the designer intended. The meticulous usage of alignment creates a design that is perfectly balanced.

Indextwo (Figure 2)

Alignment doesn't have to be taken to the extreme, and it is a self-applied rule that can be broken at times. In this site's design, we see an overall three-column layout. Each level of the design works within that. Oftentimes, the consistency from one layer to another is lost by not maintaining alignment. In the header on this site, the main navigation has broken the column structure, though the divider between two items conveniently falls on the border. This is a perfect example of breaking the rules to serve a purpose. If the designer had compressed the options into the smaller space, they would be closer and smaller, making them much more difficult to use.

Figure 1 http://www.designwithoutfrontiers.com

http://www.rawcoach.be

http://leihu.com

Figure 2 http://www.indextwo.com

http://www.onebitwonder.com

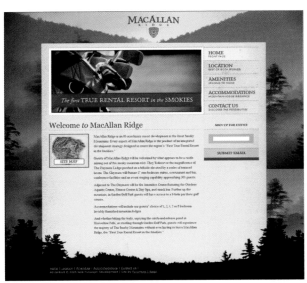

http://macallanridge.com

http://theurbanmama.com

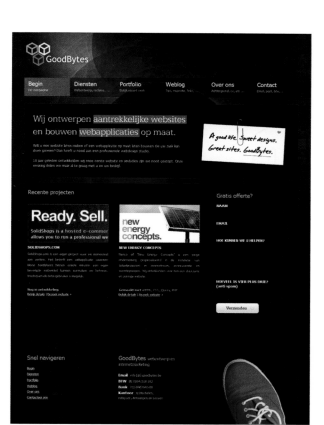

http://www.goodbytes.be

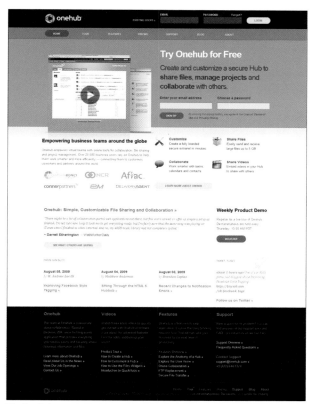

http://onehub.com

02 /
basic principles of design
emphasis • contrast • balance • alignment • **repetition** • flow

repetition

With repetition, the focus is on how elements of a design are used more than once throughout a design in varying ways. Designs that contain repetition become unified. Repetition can be achieved using many forms, including color, shape, line, fonts, imagery and an overall approach to style. This is often an inevitable design principle, because if a design has no repetition in its elements, it typically lacks a unified and cohesive feel.

A huge benefit of repetition is predictability. The user will learn to expect certain things if a site's design maintains key elements in a consistent way. All too often, a web site loses its visual cohesiveness by starting each page with a blank slate instead of developing some basic formulas to work with.

Vim Interactive (Figure 1)

In this example, there is so much repetition that it would take many pages of commentary to point them all out. I will, however, point out some of the more subtle uses of repetition. Spacing is one: Consider the amount of padding inside each container and how it matches up to the spacing elsewhere in the site. This overall consistency gives the site a very clean feel. The complexity of the dense content is reduced by this simple, hardly noticeable element. Another interesting element of the design that is heavily repeated is the pattern of larger text always having a less prominent sub text: the logo has a tagline next to it; the phone number has a statement encouraging you to use it; the large text next to the map has a smaller explanation; each "learn more" bucket has a title with sub text. This leads to the notion of predictability. In this design, the user comes to know what to expect, and the repetition is soothing.

http://www.rawsterne.co.uk

Figure 1 http://viminteractive.com

http://www.spoongraphics.co.uk

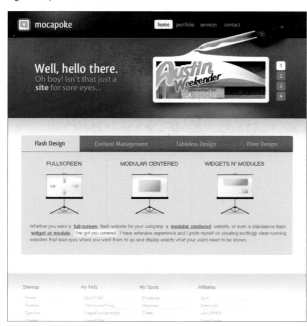

http://mocapoke.com

http://www.ukpads.com

http://www.garretthoffmann.com

http://www.nathanhackley.com

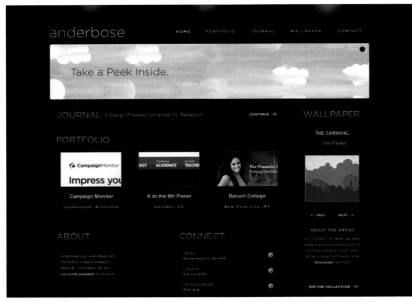

http://anderbose.com

flow

Flow is the path the user's eyes take through a design. This is primarily a result of how elements like emphasis and contrast are used. In fact, flow is entirely the result of how other elements are put together.

One thing to always remember when considering flow is the natural order of things. There have been studies that show people tend to look at things in a rather predictable fashion. Typically, a person's eyes will go from left to right and top to bottom. This is why a web site that is right-justified feels so funky to us left-to-right readers. There's nothing inherently wrong with going against the natural order; we simply must consider the implications of such decisions. The point is that it would be wise to work with the natural flow instead of trying to force something different.

Every site has a flow, good or bad. Who decides when the flow of a site is bad? When I was selecting sites as examples of good flow, I had to determine what defines good flow. This is what I settled on: I look for demonstrations of flow that feel smooth, comfortable and as natural as possible. It can be complex, but it must feel natural and comfortable so that I don't feel like I am bouncing around the page like a pinball. For me, a smooth flow is better than a rough one. A person's eyes will naturally bounce around, but a site with what I consider good flow will encourage the user to take a nice stable path, and at times it will take the person's eyes in a loop to help keep interest.

Wilson Doors (Figure 1)

This site is a nice example of comfortable flow. It doesn't hurt that the homepage is not content heavy, and there is only a small number of options. The focus starts with a large and interesting image that gives the quick elevator pitch of what they sell. From there, our eyes flow to the bottom left and across the bottom, leading us back to the main image. This clean loop makes it easy to scan and understand the options, but also to make a choice and dive in. Notice that this loop contains all the key items for the site and ensures that a user will be exposed to the option she is looking for. Also of note is the fact that the main navigation doesn't pop out. If it did, it would compete for placement in the flow and distract the user from consuming the primary set of messages.

This looping pattern is one you will find in many of the samples in this chapter. As I already mentioned, flow is the strategic combination of other design elements. This also makes flow one of the easiest elements to forget and overlook. But again, I find that if a design isn't working for me, considering this element of design can lead to the answer of why it feels broken.

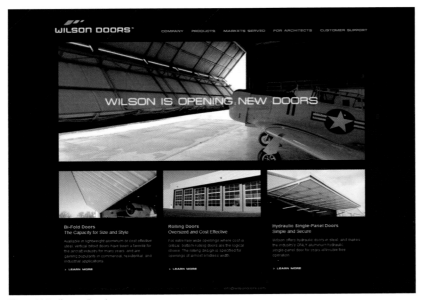

Figure 1 http://www.wilsondoors.com

http://www.recaper.com

http://www.fontex.org

http://www.gcntv.org

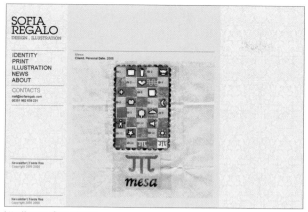

http://www.sofiaregalo.com

http://hungryhowies.com

http://garyplayer.com

http://www.digitalnoon.com

03/

iphone application • freelance • band • blog • personal • design firm • event • travel and tourism • e-commerce • business card • web utility • web software • real estate • portfolios • coming soon • t-shirt • directory

sites by type

One might think that a small set of various site types might be pointless in a book such as this, considering it would take countless volumes to cover all the basic site types there might be. But lucky for me, the goal is not to cover every potential site type. Ultimately I really have two main hopes with this section. First, I wanted to highlight some of the more active segments of the web design community (like iPhone application sites) and in that way capture some of the most popular topics of the day. Secondly, I really believe that any type of site can be inspired from any of these topics. Each has lessons to teach and each has different obstacles to overcome. These lessons and obstacles are shared with countless other topics and can easily translate over. I hope you don't skim past this part of the book if your niche isn't represented. Absorb the ideas presented by others and be inspired by them!

iphone application

iPhone applications are all the rage, and it stands to reason they will be for quite some time. They can be amazingly useful for the user, are typically very cheap if not free, and offer the opportunity for an extended impression of your brand. One key aspect of the process of building an iPhone app is the need for a beautiful design. Apple will, in fact, reject your application if it doesn't meet their design standards. So it isn't surprising to find that many of the sites set up to sell these wonderful apps look great as well.

Sites for selling these apps tend to be very focused, as they offer the opportunity to lead the user to make a quick purchase. For example, the Tea Round (Figure 1) site sells an app revolving around the making of tea. This might not give away the demographic, but it certainly reflects a common interest. As such, the site's design reflects

the audience's interests, especially in the context of tea.

Another obvious example of connecting to the target audience is the Outpost site (Figure 2). As an application that hooks into Basecamp, it only makes sense that the site connects itself as closely to Basecamp as possible; a similar color palette has been used to strengthen the connection and the site feels like a close extension of the Basecamp brand.

The designs included here have done an outstanding job at connecting to the consumers and driving them to sales. Ultimately, these are mini e-commerce sites intended to drive people to a conversion point. This explains the prominent links to Apple's App Store where the software can be purchased and downloaded. In many ways, these would be ideal candidates for a study in landing page

effectiveness and conversion rates. Why couldn't other sites be created with such focus? Portfolio sites seem like a prime candidate for such treatment.

http://libertyboom.com

Figure 1 http://tearoundapp.com

Figure 2 http://www.outpostapp.com

http://www.ticatacgames.net/static/iphone_teaser

http://www.glasshouse-apps.com

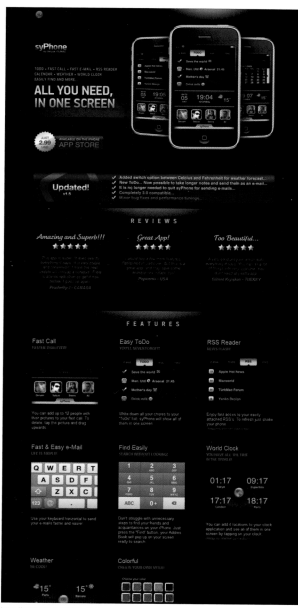

http://syphone.selcukyilmaz.com

notes from a developer

One of the most tempting things to do on a site for an iPhone application is to include a virtual iPhone to preview what the application is and does. This inevitably leads to one of three solutions:

Embedded video

Instead of trying to make a functional version of the iPhone that the user can interact with, simply embed a video to show what it does. This is best done in Flash. The embedding of the video is relatively simple; it's the video production that can run the bill up.

Flash-based emulator

If you want the user to interact with the simulated phone you will have to build a virtual iPhone in Flash. This is most likely going to be very time consuming, and it will get quickly out of date as the application gets updated.

Simple slide show

Another very common approach is a simple slide show. This is a great option to use because it is fast to build and easy to maintain, allowing for frequent updates with little to no cost.

Check out the iPhone as a Flourish chapter of this book on page 114 for more resources on building iPhone-centric designs.

http://skimaps.planetreesoftware.com

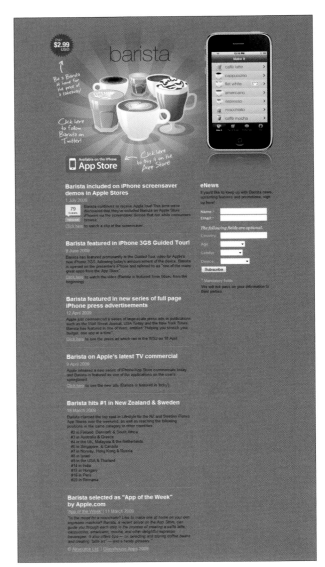

http://www.baristaapp.com

http://www.momentoapp.com

http://www.2udoku.com

http://www.thermometerapp.com

http://tapbots.com/weightbot

http://www.futuretap.com/home/whereto-en

freelance

The web site for freelancers (and web freelancers, in particular) falls somewhere between the personal portfolio site and the full design agency site. These sites must communicate not only who the individual is and what skills he or she brings to the table, but also that the person is professional and reliable. There is nothing worse than relying on a flaky freelancer.

One of the most notable samples of this niche is the site of Rob Morris, Hero for Hire (Figure 1). It seems that whenever he launches a new site, he gets all sorts of fanfare—and rightfully so. His sites are elegant, functional and just plain beautiful. His design is often imitated and even outright ripped off. So what makes his design so unique? For starters, it is exceedingly clean. The level of refinement in regard to the layout, grid structure and hierarchy is spot on. His sales pitch is clear and prominent, and the four footer buckets quickly lead you to key sections of the site.

David James's site (Figure 2) accomplishes many of the same things with a totally different approach. Here, it is more about a flow of portfolio pieces. Yet the site is highly organized, easy to consume and reflective of the high level of his professionalism.

Another interesting example of a freelancer site is Traxor Designs (Figure 3). What is striking about this design is the prominent use of a clear sales pitch. This is an industry saturated with a variety of niches and specific skill sets. In this case the quick sales pitch sums up the individual's core skills and lets the visitor know that he focuses on design and SEO work. This sort of precise communication can help attract exactly the type of work a freelancer wants.

Ronnie San (Figure 4) takes a similar approach with his prominent "your website, simplified" statement. He knows that building a site is complicated and painful for those who don't know how. So he attempts to position himself apart from the herd and give consumers a reason to work with him by appealing to their desire to have a painless experience building a web site.

Figure 1 http://www.digitalmash.com

Figure 2 http://www.djgd.co.uk

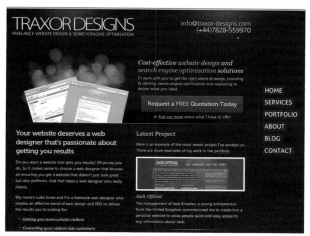

Figure 3 http://www.traxor-designs.com

Figure 4 http://www.ronniesan.com

http://www.patrickmonkel.nl

http://madebyelephant.com

http://www.lynncyr.com

http://www.zivmeltzer.com

http://www.brizk.com

http://petehellyer.com

http://larkef.com

http://ryanplesko.com

sites by type

iphone application • freelance • **band** • blog • personal • design firm • event • travel and tourism • e-commerce •
business card • web utility • web software • real estate • portfolios • coming soon • t-shirt • directory

band

If you ever want to do an interesting design experiment, band web sites create a distinct opportunity. Look at the web sites for some bands that you are wholly unfamiliar with. Based on what you see on the sites, make a quick list of the ways you would describe the music you suspect they produce.

Music puts off a clear mood, style and tempo (along with a dozen other ways to describe it). Site designs also put off various aesthetics. A great test of a design is to see if these styles match.

In my examples, I am not so concerned about this matchup as I am about the various trends being followed in this niche. One thing that becomes abundantly clear in this industry is the effectiveness of social media, especially when we remind ourselves that MySpace had its roots in promoting bands. Nearly every example of band sites will point to MySpace, Facebook and various other networks, often in a very prominent place on the page. Could it be that one of the most important roles a site like this could play is to get people to friend you on social sites? It would seem so, based on the prime real estate these icons occupy.

Another common denominator among these sites is the need for a visual style or language. Some are graphically intense (as on Goodbye Elliott's site, Figure 1), some are exceedingly stylistic (as on the Still Rain site, Figure 2) while others seem to be purely decorative.

Based on their sites, branding is a huge issue for many bands. Making the band name the largest and most dominant element of the page is common for relatively unknown (or up-and-coming) bands. As an example, on the site for The Iveys (Figure 3), the band name and its framework takes up nearly a full screen of space.

Sometimes there is a temptation to do something radical with a design and create something experimental to portray a band's "new" or "unique" style. But wise designers of these sites follow deliberate patterns that function to make finding out about these bands a simple process.

http://betterplacerecordings.com

Figure 1 http://www.goodbyeelliott.com

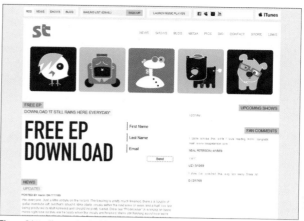

Figure 2 http://www.standardthompson.com

Figure 3 http://www.theiveysmusic.com

notes from a developer

Specific niches like this inevitably lead to many common elements in site design. That is to say, the content of these sites are all very, very similar. Many bands were drawn to MySpace in its early days because it was easy to use and let them spread the word and share their music. There are countless site-building systems, many of which are targeted at specific niches. Such is the case with the music industry.

A perfect example of this is ebandlive.com. Several of the samples in this chapter are built on this platform. I bring this up because leveraging a tool such as this can be a great way to streamline the building of a band's web site. This works best if you plan for this and create the design around the available functionality. Given that most bands are not bloated with extra cash to pay web developers, this is a great way to help your clients get lots of functionality for their money. Even better, it leaves a bit more of the budget to be used for design time, meaning better-looking end results.

http://www.rocketclub.info

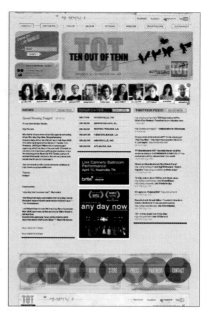

http://10outoftenn.com

http://www.dimmn.com

http://www.jazzforme.de

http://www.sickcityclub.net

http://sourhaze.com/ep1

http://www.muddriverunion.com/index.htm

http://www.marianastrench.net

03 / sites by type

iphone application • freelance • band • **blog** • personal • design firm • event • travel and tourism • e-commerce •
business card • web utility • web software • real estate • portfolios • coming soon • t-shirt • directory

blog

Blogging is a vital element in the next generation of the Internet. Inherently, blogging builds on a community of readers. As with any web site, you have a small window of time to capture the attention of the user. What follows are a few key considerations when designing a blog to ensure the blog's message is effectively delivered.

Add Images to Get Posts Read

Blog strategists talk about the creation of short, catchy blog post titles. While this is an effective tip for increasing consumption of your content, another thing you can do to grab a user's eyes is add images or graphics to all your posts. Each graphic needs to be exciting, dramatic and related to the content of the post. Inspired Mag (Figure 1) creates custom graphics for every one of their posts. Design Shard (Figure 2) uses screenshots to show the effectiveness of their tutorials. The Statement (Figure 3) incorporates several graphics or photos, effectively creating a gallery of related images for each post.

Make Feature Articles Stand Out

Whether it is with a simple border, a change in color, or a graphic element, you can draw a user's eyes to a specific section of a site. There, you should feature your most recent or most popular articles. idsgn (Figure 4) uses an increase in image size and placement to push their most recent article. Upsidestudio (Figure 5) shows only their most recent blog post on the homepage. Snook (Figure 6) simply separates the featured article from the rest with bolded and enlarged text and a small change in placement.

Make It Easy, Make It Fast

Whether you're designing a "mommy blog" or a corporate news blog, the end game is the same; a thriving blog needs users subscribing, commenting and sharing.

Figure 1 http://www.inspiredm.com

Make it easy on the user—help him reach a goal by using obvious and traditional placements of graphics and links.

Subscribing: The RSS icon has become a staple in blog design and should always have a place at the top, center and bottom of every blog. A simple click of the icon should bring up a feed or a feed page that features several ways for a user to subscribe. Upsidestudio (Figure 5), for example, has several conveniently placed RSS icons throughout their design.

Commenting: Every post should have a link leading directly to the comment submission form. Entice the user by showing the comment count or stating "Be the first to comment." Readers want to either join in on a conversation taking place or be the first to share their opinions.

Sharing: Along with comment links, every post should have a simple way to share its URL on social networks. Typically, the logo of the social network is used as a link and once clicked, a user will be brought to that site with content related to the post already filled out and ready to share.

Figure 2 http://www.designshard.com

Figure 3 http://www.theoldstate.com/blog

Figure 4 http://www.idsgn.org

Figure 5 http://upsidestudio.com

Figure 6 http://snook.ca

notes from a developer

As a developer, one of the most painful things to get from a designer is some crazy conceptual way to visualize a blog. So often, these visualizations of data are inflexible and immensely complicated, and they always require fancy transitions. The frustration happens when these grand ideas are paired with the realities of how tools like WordPress and other blog platforms are actually built.

In a niche such as this, the designer who has never coded anything often produces designs that are problematic and expensive. Your best bet as a designer is to think simple (though well-designed, of course) and focus on making it easy for the user to consume the data.

As a designer, you would be well served to implement a design or two as a WordPress theme and see the limitations of how a dynamic site works. I guarantee the people designing amazing WordPress templates have built their own and thoroughly understand the limitations.

http://razvanphotography.com

http://www.havocinspired.co.uk

PRETTY SKETCHY

2009 Apr 22 · COMMENTS ♡ 63 · PUBLISHED IN Design, Thinking · ← PREV

I SEEM TO BE GETTING INTO MANY CONVERSATIONS LATELY ON THE MERITS OF KEEPING A SKETCHBOOK. ALMOST EVERYONE AGREES THEY ARE A GOOD IDEA, BUT SURPRISINGLY FEW ACTUALLY DO IT. THE EXCUSE I HEAR MOST OFTEN FROM NON-SKETCHERS IS "I CAN'T DRAW." AND NOW I'LL TELL YOU WHAT I TOLD THEM:

★ SKETCHBOOKS ARE NOT ABOUT BEING A GOOD ARTIST, THEY'RE ABOUT BEING A GOOD THINKER.

OBVIOUSLY, SOME PEOPLE DO BRING THE PRACTICE OF SKETCHING TO A HIGHER ART FORM, BUT TO ME IT'S ALWAYS BEEN ABOUT VISUAL BRAINSTORMING AND RECORD-KEEPING IN A FORMAT WITH A RIDICULOUSLY LOW BARRIER TO ENTRY. MY DRAWINGS LOOK LIKE SHIT, BUT FIDELITY DOESN'T MATTER AS LONG AS I CAN CONVEY MY IDEAS TO OTHERS OR TO MY FUTURE SELF.

WE SHOULD REVEL IN NOT CARING HOW GOOD OR BAD WE ARE, AND BY KNOWING THAT WE HONE OUR CREATIVITY WITH EACH STROKE OF THE PENCIL. THE POINT IS TO KEEP DOING, IT'S HOW YOU GET STUFF DONE. AND MOST CERTAINLY HOW YOU GET BETTER.

I'M TRYING TO GET MYSELF INTO THE HABIT OF FILLING UP A PAGE OR SO A DAY. SOMETIMES THIS MIGHT JUST BE A LIST OF THOUGHTS, OTHER TIMES IT'S A DRAWING OR A BUNCH OF THUMBNAILS. I DON'T CARE IF PRACTICE MAKES PERFECT, I'M HAPPY IF PRACTICE KEEPS ME COMPETENT.

IN THE SPIRIT OF AWARENESS, I'VE SET UP A flickr GROUP FOR THIS VERY PURPOSE. POST ONE, AND ONLY ONE, SPREAD/PAGE FROM YOUR SKETCHBOOK. IT'S ALWAYS FUN TO SEE HOW EVERYONE ELSE'S MIND WORKS.

COMMENTS ♡ 63 · DESIGN TAGS Beige, Black, Hand-drawn Type, Illustration · ← PREV

ON THE SUBJECT OF ME
Jason Santa Maria is a graphic designer based and working in sunny Brooklyn, NY. MORE ↓

RECENT PROJECTS

ALL PROJECTS →

RSS FEEDS
■ Articles
■ Oddities & Diversions
■ Daily Photography

DAILY PHOTOGRAPHY

COMMENTARY ♡ 2 · ARCHIVE

WITH SUPPORT FROM
(mt)
Ads Via The Deck

SEARCH THE SITE
SEARCH

ODDITIES & DIVERSIONS

WOOD TYPE MUSEUM
Wood Type Museum, does of beautiful type and specimens books. Peruse or get lost. Via H&FJ. News who have a great post on Hamilton's Wood Type Catalog #14 →

A NEW TYPOGRAPHICA
Typographica redesigns and it's simply beautiful. Don't miss the latest feature on their Favorite Typefaces of 2008 →

A LIST APART ISSUE 282
A List Apart Issue 282. Can we finally get real type on the web? Don't beauty in design have a benefit besides aesthetic pleasure? Interview with David Berlow by Jeffrey Zeldman and an article by Stephen P. Anderson →

PAST ODDITIES & DIVERSIONS →

RECOMMENDED READING
How To Be a Graphic Designer Without Losing Your Soul
by Adrian Shaughnessy

ALL BOOKS →

http://jasonsantamaria.com

Beyondjazz
online future jazz · since 2003

search

home · podcast · articles
elsewhere · news · about

domu '99-'01 tribute

Domu leaves the music industry, but not before we tune into the amazing early productions that defined his sound!

Beyondjazz - for any music lover with a passion for broken beats, hiphop, house, nujazz, funk, soul, dubstep ...

podcast

#360 – Newness
Sun 10 Jan 10 - by lensco · 8 Comments

A new year and a new studio for urgent.fm - yay! But for the playlist though, we used the same old recipe - tried and tested - of nujazz, hiphop, house, broken beats and a dash of dubstep.

Note: the quality of this recording may be a bit under par, as the new studio isn't fully set up yet. Still, enjoy!

◄ ► ■

download me mp3
Build An Ark – Sweet Thing – Kindred Spirits
Sun Ra & His Outer Space Arkestra – Nuclear War – Soul Jazz
Bennson – Uto (ft. Willow Nelson) – Raw Fusion
Landau Orchestra – Conceptions – Raw Canvas
The Louie Gee Ensemble – You Belong With Me ft. Monique Harcum – LDBK
Silhouette Brown – Leave A Note – 2000Black
Dwele – Eve (I Need You) – Rewor"k" The Art Inc.

Gonja Sufi – Ancestors – Warp
Jar Moff – Untitled – CDR
Daisuke Tanabe – Kanon – Circulations
Nosaj Thing – Distro – Nosaj Thing
10-20 – Endzone – Highpoint Lowlife
Tikie – SL 1200' – demo
Dynooo – Tranch – MacFly
Vikter Duplaix – Electric Love (Nicolay Remix) – vikterduplaix.com
Raoul Lambert – 3 Seconds – We Play House

Jazzanova – Look What You're Doin' To Me (Motor City Drum Ensemble Remix) – Universal
Joy Orbison – Hyph Mngo (Andreas Saag's House Perspective) – none
Comfort Fit – Bit By Bit (Philta's TechBruk Rehook) – none
Live Tropical Fish – Rubber Soul (Domu Remix) – Live Tropical Fish
Altered Natives – Rass Out – Fresh Minute Music
Pocketknife ft. Joe Worricker – Get Around To It (Mark E Remix) – Electric Minds

Equal i's – Babylon – demo
Ke$ha – Tik Tok (Untold Remix Dub) – Jive
MJ Cole – Sanctuary (Sbtrkt Remix) – none
2562 – Flashback – Tectonic
José James – Emotions – Brownswood

Here's oemebamo getting acquainted with the new studio (cell phone pic):

articles

Shortcuts: Four Tet, José James

home · podcast · articles
elsewhere · news · about

recently
podcast · #360 – Newness
articles · Shortcuts: Four Tet, José James and Silhouette Brown
articles · Best In Music 2009 – Lensco
podcast · #359 – Sun Sods in studio
podcast · #358 – Beyondjazz meets World Service

supported by What's this?
5 FREE DOWNLOADS
advertise here?

subscribe to the podcast
Never miss another episode of the Beyondjazz radioshow by grabbing the podcast feed and popping it into your favorite podcast app!
podcast feed · subscribe with iTunes

beyondjazz on twitter What's this?
beyondjazz @ katikawoel drops new album (+ freebies) via www.redfurbinanacademy.com/london &blog?id=1205
beyondjazz: RT @RUMA, London 2010 site now live. Yeah, http://www.redfurbmusicacademy.com/
Gerard Drive By: RT @beyondjazz: RT @nipandadump: XLRBR podcast : Motor City Drum Ensemble http://bit.ly &BB4bq >looking fwd to checking this
beyondjazz: RT @nipandadump: XLRBR podcast : Motor City Drum Ensemble http //bit.ly/8BB4bq
beyondjazz: RT @redtest: New blog post: MastForce - Clear Thru U http //bit.ly/6UT8J

Follow @beyondjazz on Twitter

flickr group

recent comments
cremrisal on Shortcuts: Four Tet, José James and Silhouette Brown
oemebamo on Shortcuts: Four Tet, José James and Silhouette Brown
lensco on Shortcuts: Four Tet, José James and Silhouette Brown
Denn Dupardin on Best In Music 2009 – Lensco
Funky D on #358 - Beyondjazz meets WorldService

© 2003-2010 beyondjazz
designed by @oemebamo

brand new!

http://beyondjazz.net

http://exp.horizontal.mykl.nl

http://roquealonso.org

sites by type

iphone application • freelance • band • blog • **personal** • design firm • event • travel and tourism • e-commerce •
business card • web utility • web software • real estate • portfolios • coming soon • t-shirt • directory

personal

The very idea of a personal web site harkens back to the earliest days of the Internet, a time when people with web sites were uber nerds and most people had no idea how to even look at them. The personal site has since become very commonplace. A combination of WordPress and a few key plug-ins can quickly get you a nice, easy-to-update site. Hook in some Flickr, Last.fm and a dash of Twitter, and people can learn all they care to about you.

This is what sets a personal site apart from a portfolio site or a more business-focused one. It offers a chance to get to know the individual a bit more, and it has not only a professional appeal, but also a personal one that entices family and friends to stay in touch and up to date on the person's latest adventures.

At Chris Sloan's web site (Figure 1), we find the home of a designer and developer.

We see the typical portfolio pieces, but the incorporation of more personal elements transition this site into this niche. Probably the best part of a site like this is how many aspects update automatically. Also note the social media links that enable his readers to connect with him on their preferred social network.

Another fun demonstration of this niche (and one devoid of any business aspects) is the personal site of Trist and Jen Chiappisi (Figure 2). This wedding site turned personal site offers a chance for the new couple to share their life with family and friends. While these sites might have a limited audience and purpose, their functionality is still critical. Consider the wide age range of readers, and you are quickly reminded that usability is key (as is readability, so no tiny text here).

Whether you're starting a site for your new baby or you want a semi-personal

professional site to show yourself to the world, this set of sites will provide a range of solutions showcasing what others have come up with.

http://www.havocinspired.co.uk

Figure 1 http://chrissloan.info

Figure 2 http://www.chiappisi.com

http://www.jasongraphix.com

http://www.joedowdle.com

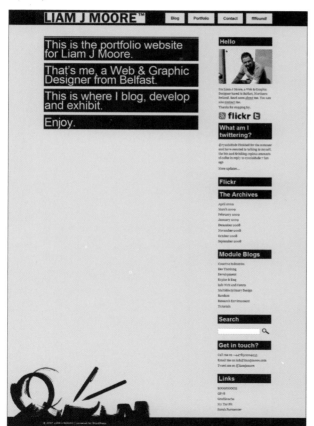

http://benjaminminnich.com

http://www.liamjmoore.com

notes from a developer

Personal sites might be more focused on the personal side of life, but that's not to say there isn't a place for some basic business stuff. In particular, I am thinking of an online resume. This makes good sense when you consider employers frequently look up potential employees online as a part of the recruiting process.

With that in mind, there are a few great solutions that will help you quickly create a beautiful online resume. Krop.com now offers resume building, as does ceevee.com and innovativeresume.com.

When you find yourself in dire need of a resume and want to post it online, chances are you don't want to wait on your programmer friend to help you, and you don't want to slop something together (it is your resume, after all). In such times, tools like these will help you quickly build a beautiful resume that will represent you well online.

http://www.neboo5.net

http://www.allaboutchris.co.uk

http://www.tjmapes.com

03 / **sites by type**

iphone application • freelance • band • blog • personal • **design firm** • event • travel and tourism • e-commerce • business card • web utility • web software • real estate • portfolios • coming soon • t-shirt • directory

design firm

Most people who have launched their own personal sites know that it can be a daunting task. It is not uncommon to hear that people have gone through half a dozen variations before getting totally exasperated and just launching something to get it done. It seems that unlimited possibilities lead to an inevitable stalemate of the brain, from which we designers have a hard time escaping. If you imagine that you have a whole team of people with an unlimited range of possibilities, you are envisioning a situation prime for frustration. This is an issue every agency faces: What will our public image be?

These internal hurdles make it all the more remarkable when you find agency sites that function well and present an appealing message to their consumers. One such example is the site for the agency Grow (Figure 1). This site makes use of a common style found in agency sites these days: minimalism. A well-designed minimal style lets the work shine and highlights the agency's ability to make even something relatively simple beautiful.

Another highly functional design firm example is the Paramore Redd web site (Figure 2). This site demonstrates a focus on quick communication and simplicity to reinforce the minimalist mindset. In this case, they espouse a focus on results, and as such, a minimalistic style meshes very well with this singular focus.

In stark contrast, the site for Saizen Media Studios (Figure 3) shows that a far more visual solution can also be effective. The logic of demonstrating their focus remains the same though, and the site's style closely matches the Flash-centric and highly visual sites they build. Given their portfolio, it would be very confusing to find a minimal site without the agency's usual visual fanfare.

http://komodomedia.com

Figure 1 http://www.thisisgrow.com

Figure 3 http://www.saizenmedia.com

http://www.syck.com

Figure 2 http://paramoreredd.com

http://www.aspect-webdesign.com

http://www.24-7media.de

http://madebyrocket.com

http://definecreative.com.au

http://www.zaum.co.uk

http://www.thinkcw.com

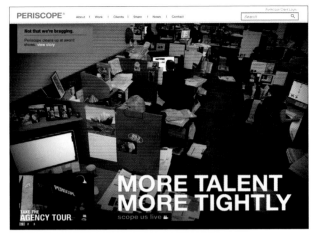

http://www.periscope.com

http://www.area17.com

http://junecloud.com

sites by type

iphone application • freelance • band • blog • personal • design firm • **event** • travel and tourism • e-commerce • business card • web utility • web software • real estate • portfolios • coming soon • t-shirt • directory

event

Event sites seem to follow a fairly common pattern. The sites in this niche tend to be graphic heavy (as in, the designs rely on lots of images) and are often very thematic. Not surprisingly, these themes tend to echo the topic of the event. Considering the diversity of topics presented in the following examples, it is amazing the designers have all found a similar style.

For example, let's consider the Portage County Randolph Fair site (Figure 1). I have been to some county fairs, and I must say I am extremely impressed at the quality of this fair's web site. The design is not over-the-top, but it certainly echoes the all-American, down-to-earth wholesomeness that can be found at such events. It's slightly patriotic, with a touch of vintage.

The site for a lecture series from the American Marketing Association (Figure 2)

takes an approach that also relies on imagery to convey the theme of the event. While the visual style is totally different from the fair's, the purpose of both sites is the same. They convey what to expect and the atmosphere that will likely exist. In this case, the site looks hip and trendy, suggesting it is truly the latest information on the topic, not rehashed ideas from five years ago.

Let's compare those sites with the Pecha Kucha site (Figure 3). This event is geared toward creatives, and the site's design clearly reflects that.

It seems the design of an event site inevitably echoes what the audience would like to see at the event. Is this really all that surprising, though? This is one of those situations where it only makes sense to play into expectations. You don't see any off-the-wall navigation styles here, just usable and clear designs.

Figure 1 http://www.randolphfair.com

Figure 2 http://www.uabama.com/lectures

http://www.festivalboreal.com

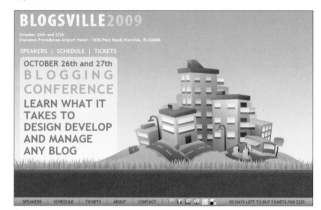

http://blogsville.us

Figure 3 http://www.doyoupk.org

http://www.therustyball.com

http://summercamp.carsonified.com

http://naias.com

notes from a developer

If you're planning an event and are interested in creating a web site to help promote the event, chances are you are going to ask your developer about implementing an online registration system.

But before you jump in, you should realize that this may be a bit of a daunting task. Sure, a simple solution could be coded and built, but if you're expecting a large number of attendees or if you have some complex variables associated with the event, chances are this will be more difficult and expensive than you might think.

This is not to discourage you from pursuing such ideas, but rather to help you realize what you're in for. In fact, there are whole businesses built around the notion of event management. Two nice tools for this niche are eventbrite. com and epicevent.com.

http://www.reelrocktour.com

http://stackoverflow.carsonified.com

http://www.visitsalford.info/foodfestival

03 / **sites by type**
iphone application • freelance • band • blog • personal • design firm • event • **travel and tourism** • e-commerce •
business card • web utility • web software • real estate • portfolios • coming soon • t-shirt • directory

travel and tourism

For as big an industry as travel and tourism represents, it's amazing how difficult it can be to find good information online. Perhaps it is the various conflicting commercial interests—like which restaurant should be first on a list—or the mere fact that people will travel to Florida regardless of the lack of good web sites. There are plenty of good information sources outside the web, and travel is a niche that books have most thoroughly covered.

It's easy to shop and compare airfare, hotels and rental cars, but it is not nearly as easy to shop for other amenities such as local attractions or kid-friendly restaurants. In planning a recent trip to Florida, I was severely unimpressed by the availability of good information on the web. One would think that with rabid popularity of services like yelp.com or Google maps that finding fun things to do would be far easier than it really is. Fortunately there are some positive examples to contradict this frustration. Let's dig in and see just how this niche can be accomplished successfully.

Perhaps the most forward-thinking of the examples here is the site for Oklahoma City's Bricktown (Figure 1). Not only do you get to browse the downtown area for various amenities, but the interface itself provides more than just a list of options. With images and useful information online, you get an immediate idea of the atmosphere of various locations. You also get to see each feature's geographic location, which helps with planning what is near your hotel, or what is easily accessible.

It's like a super-deluxe version of Google Maps catering to out-of-town travelers.

A more traditional example of this niche can be found on the Savour Durham site (Figure 2). Here, you're guided to clear buckets of information (calendar, maps, tickets), and the commercial elements are fairly obvious with the logos at the bottom. The latter is really nice, because it can be confusing to figure out whether space is purchased on a site versus when its location is merited based on the quality of the product. In other words, any crappy restaurant can purchase a prominent placement, but that is not nearly as useful as a third party rating it as such. The point is that it is always nice have a clear separation between sharing valuable information and paid listings on a site.

Figure 1 http://www.welcometobricktown.com

Figure 2 http://www.gatesopen.ca

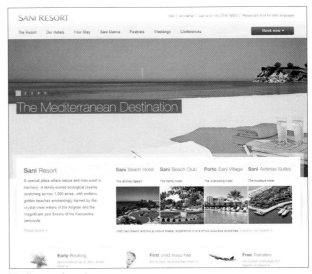

http://www.sani-resort.com

http://www.definitelydubai.com

http://www.campingilfrutteto.it

http://www.amsterdam-bed-and-breakfasts.com

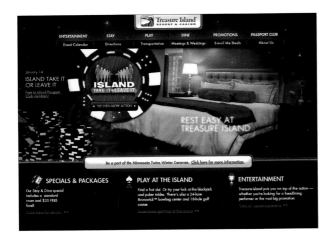

http://treasureislandcasino.com

http://www.paristaylorhotel.com

http://www.barceloraval.com

http://www.trappfamily.com

http://www.icystraitpoint.com

03 / sites by type
iphone application • freelance • band • blog • personal • design firm • event • travel and tourism • **e-commerce** •
business card • web utility • web software • real estate • portfolios • coming soon • t-shirt • directory

e-commerce

Perhaps more than any other type of web site, e-commerce sites are driven by raw numbers. This form of commerce is unique because exact results can be measured: For example, the amount of effort that would be required to track every single visitor to a Walmart store and what they look at is astronomical, but with every web site comes log files that can reveal mountains of information about users' actions. Change the color of a button, and you can measure how much sales change. As such, there is less of a drive to attain a beautiful design (for design's sake) on e-commerce sites and more of a focus on results. With this in mind, it is impressive to find some remarkably beautiful designs in this chapter. While this chapter will not attempt to suggest what might produce the most sales, it can offer some ideas that may work for you, and look good doing so.

Sloppy is perhaps the best word to describe the majority of e-commerce sites. Minimal is one of the least likely, but Asphaltgold (Figure 1) is one such example. This type of site needs so many elements to function, and a minimalist approach is not typically one that gets considered. Therefore, the minimal style of this site is rather unusual. Much like a portfolio site, this design almost elevates shoes to works of art. Considering this site's uber-stylish approach, this makes perfect sense. Not only is the approach extremely practical from a maintenance standpoint, but it clearly represents exactly the type of experience their potential consumers would expect.

In contrast to this minimalist style, yayadog.com (Figure 2) demonstrates that a far more distinct and stylized approach can function just as well. Again, the site's design connects perfectly with the product and the audience it speaks to. This demonstrates a huge upside to not being a mega store: the ability to focus. By focusing on a smaller, more targeted audience, the site can more effectively connect and convert them to sales.

The quantity of products e-commerce sites offer can vary greatly. For example, the ReadyHang (Figure 3) site has a single product. With such a radically small range of product to represent, a totally different layout can be leveraged. In this case, it is more about the sales pitch of why you should be using the Ready-Hang products instead of the traditional options. Streamlined communication and attention to detail make for an impressive sales pitch.

Figure 1 http://www.asphaltgold.de

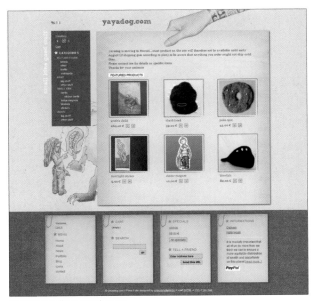

Figure 2 http://www.yayadog.com

Figure 3 http://www.readyhang.com

http://www.letscollect.co.uk

http://www.threadless.com

One of the questions I get all the time is: "I have something I want to sell online—how can I make it happen?" And, of course, hideous visions of insanely complex e-commerce systems come to mind. After I calm down and tell them they are poking into the most complex type of web site possible, I remind myself there are some super-slick tools now that make this a painless process.

In fact, when I decided to sell my first book myself, I set up a shop via bigcartel.com. In no less than a couple hours, I had set up a shop, applied my logo and colors and loaded up my product, and I was open for business. Now that is what I call simple.

Big Cartel isn't the only solution out there to creating an effective and nice-looking e-commerce site; shopify.com is another super simple one.

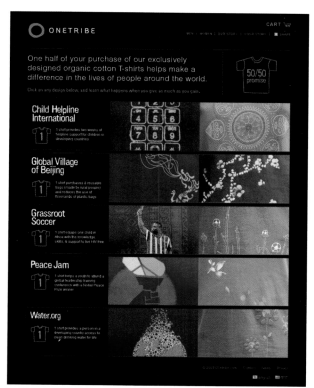

http://www.onetribe.com

http://www.twelvesouth.com

http://ridefourever.com

http://www.creativesoutfitter.com

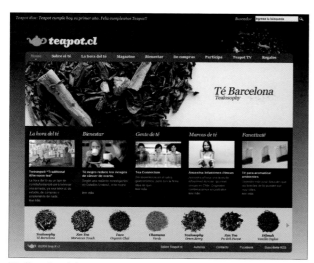

http://www.teapot.cl

http://jaqkcellars.com

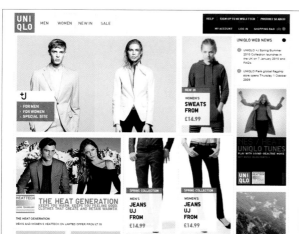

http://www.uniqlo.co.uk

http://www.matthewwilliamson.com

03 / **sites by type**
iphone application • freelance • band • blog • personal • design firm • event • travel and tourism • e-commerce •
business card • web utility • web software • real estate • portfolios • coming soon • t-shirt • directory

business card

The name pretty much says it all. Following a theme of minimalism (in content) and a frequently tiny amount of space, business card sites sum things up rather quickly. As with a real business card, these sites present a small amount of information in a concise and direct way.

Deciding to design such a simple site can happen for many reasons, from a need to simply communicate a small amount of information to a lack of time to flesh out a larger site. Whatever the case, these tiny packages can be incredibly effective. Even though business cards are small, I never find myself wishing a business card contained some extra bit of information; everything I need is always there. Such is the case with these sites.

In the micro site for Tim Van Damme (Figure 1), we see a style he started that is being rapidly copied, which is a sign of an effective design. Instead of adding more content to the pile on this landing page, Tim simply points to all of the social networks and public online applications he uses. In this way, the site is like a distributed and highly specialized content system.

Another fine example can be found on the Appenstein site (Figure 2). Here, the individual's name isn't included, but other key elements, like a phone number and key skills, are highlighted. In a world short of iPhone developers, the site's owner need not say more to get plenty of attention.

One of the more distinct examples is that of Waqas Ashraf (Figure 3). Here, we only get a skills summary and a link to contact the person. Does this individual have a lack of information and portfolio pieces to share? Or is he simply to the point and efficient with his time and efforts?

http://www.leandaryan.com

http://www.jonwardweb.co.uk

Figure 1 http://timvandamme.com

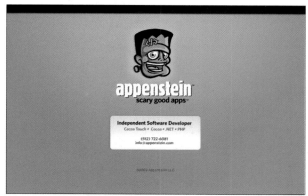

Figure 2 http://appenstein.com

Figure 3 http://waqasashraf.com

http://www.jordankeating.com

http://www.ultimate-mediagroup.nl

http://andycroll.com

notes from a developer

If you're looking to have a business card–style web site, you will most likely be implementing the end product yourself. I suppose a business might pay someone to do this, but for the most part, this style is really geared toward personal landing pages.

As such, you will likely realize that simple-looking effects like accordions and moving icons are a lot more complex than you might imagine, as you must piece together HTML, CSS and JavaScript for a pleasing end result. Luckily, there is a free WordPress template at http://templatic.com/demo/visitingcard/#networks that allows you to quickly implement a site in this style. If you're an ambitious designer (or a seasoned coder), this is a fantastic starting point that can easily be modified to have almost any look and feel while retaining functionality.

http://rogieking.com

http://brisdom.com/evertslagter

http://bitminers.com

03 / sites by type

iphone application • freelance • band • blog • personal • design firm • event • travel and tourism • e-commerce •
business card • **web utility** • web software • real estate • portfolios • coming soon • t-shirt • directory

web utility

Web utilities are tools (typically hosted solutions) that offer a specific set of functionality. For example, SonarHQ (Figure 1) offers the ability to do online surveys, Cee-Vee (Figure 2) is a focused resume builder, and WROI (Figure 3) is a link-tracking tool on steroids. These apps offer a piece of functionality that will eventually be a small component of a web site, instead of the entire solution like a hosted e-commerce or blog system might.

One element these sites share is that the extreme focus of their functionality offers a quick sales pitch opportunity. For example, SonarHQ has four large words on its homepage: Create your survey site. You hardly have to read any more to know what they offer—good, old-fashioned surveys. CeeVee does something similar, though they could have made it in two words: online resumes. The point is that

with such a focus, you can quickly explain yourself. If you don't do so, you risk losing the attention of your visitors.

Shortwave (Figure 4) makes use of a thin single column format, a layout that is becoming very rare these days. With the increasing popularity of wide-screen monitors, thin, single-column sites are a thing of the past. This site reminds us that if we don't have a lot of information to communicate, it might make sense to streamline it and not try to fluff it up to be something bigger than what it actually is. The situation is comparable to the single-man freelance shop trying to pretend to be a bigger agency. Why pretend? Embrace what you are. In this case, you're a focused web utility that can survive with an extremely concise marketing presence.

Stay Valid (Figure 5) comes pretty close to doing the same thing as Shortwave—

keeping things simple and to the point, at least in the header part of the homepage. It quickly says what it does and encourages you to just try it. No complex sales pitch needed. The user need only be directed toward the conversion point.

http://thurlyapp.com

Figure 1 http://www.sonarhq.com

Figure 2 http://ceevee.com

Figure 3 http://www.w3roi.com

Figure 4 http://shortwaveapp.com

Figure 5 http://www.stayvalid.com

http://wufoo.com

http://heywatch.com

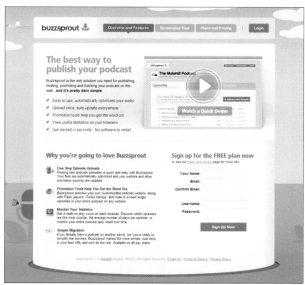

http://www.buzzsprout.com

◎③ / **sites by type**

iphone application • freelance • band • blog • personal • design firm • event • travel and tourism • e-commerce •
business card • web utility • **web software** • real estate • portfolios • coming soon • t-shirt • directory

web software

In contrast to web utilities, this type of site typically offers a full set of functionality, which represents either a full web site or a service that doesn't get plugged in to another system. Surveys, for example, typically fit into another site, while hosted e-commerce systems like Kartel (Figure 1) and LemonStand (Figure 2) offer an application that operates as an entire web site. Others, like Campaign Monitor (Figure 3) and The Invoice Machine (Figure 4), offer hosted online services for specific functionality that isn't necessarily a component of a public-facing web site.

One thing these sites share with web utilities sites is their focus and the opportunity to quickly sell users on what they do. Every example here contains a quick sales pitch to inform the user of what she is looking at. This has become a critical element of such sites, and the pattern is seen over and over again.

The big difference in the needs of the user of a web software site versus a web utilities site is the inevitable need for more information. These bits of information connect closely with a user's desire to take steps towards being a paying customer. For example, does the e-commerce software support drop shipping? Does your e-mail service offer e-mail testing? Functionality questions come into play as key factors that determine a consumer's level of interest.

LemonStand is a perfect example of a focus on answering questions before they are asked. The homepage offers a quick "here is what it does" sort of message with two key action items: take a tour and get a beta download. The part of the page below that has a lower position in the hierarchy and is far more content heavy. It offers a few key bits of information that serve as the main selling points. For example, flexibility and extendibility stand out from the copy as key elements of the software. It stands to reason that Lemon-Stand would showcase its strengths, or at least turn their weaknesses into strengths by making them selling points. (This is a bit off track, but it is a common sales approach. Consider Coke Classic instead of the old Coke we have always had. Coke Classic is a positive spin on what might be considered a weakness.) The point is that the homepage for this site could be a one-sheet flyer for quickly selling the product and answering key questions.

This approach could be applied to many other niches, such as personal portfolios, agency web sites and typical product sites, all of which present situations where we are often prone to showing pretty images and not necessarily addressing key points.

Figure 1 http://www.kartel.co.nz

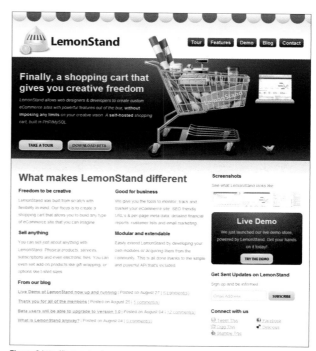

Figure 2 http://lemonstandapp.com

Figure 3 http://www.campaignmonitor.com

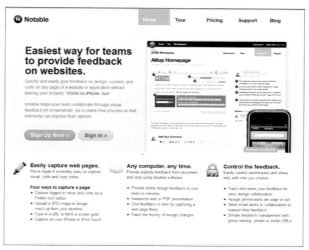

http://www.notableapp.com

Figure 4 http://invoicemachine.com

http://feedafever.com

notes from a developer

As a designer working on a software product, one of the most responsible things you can do is consider usability. Quite often, designers come to me with ideas of some crazy type of interface to accomplish a task. More often than not, the functionality they describe could be done with a simple standard control (like a drop-down, check box or slider control). Sometimes the desire to be creative and different can be counterproductive and radically increase costs.

As a diligent designer, one of the most practical things you can do is familiarize yourself with the various interface widgets available. Ui-patterns.com is a great resource for doing just that.

Another extremely useful tool in this area is software to help you with usability testing. When you start to look at how users respond to interfaces, you start to understand how important it is to make this clear and simple. Silverback (silverbackapp.com) is a great tool that happens to be really cheap; a more expensive but feature-filled option is TechSmith's Morae (http://www.techsmith.com/morae.asp).

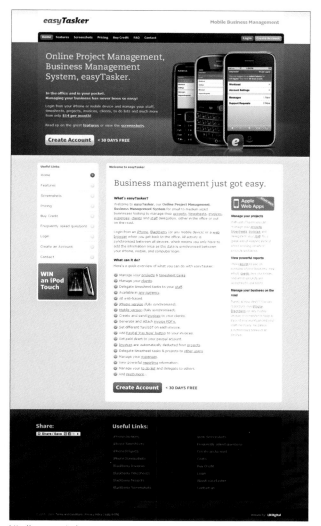

http://www.easytasker.com

http://www.cubescripts.com

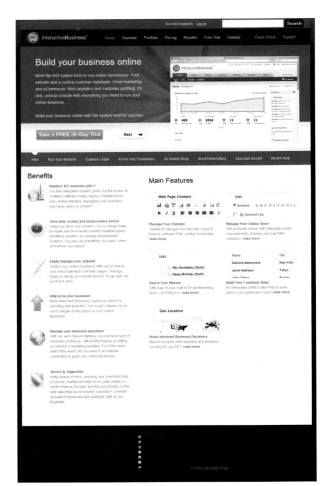

http://www.interactive-business.com.au

http://www.splash360.com

real estate

This is a niche that typically has incredibly low standards, but I am excited to show a series of sites that demonstrate that it is possible to have a great site in this industry.

One particular aspect of this set of sites that strikes me is how they so clearly appeal to their target demographic. Well, I presume it is their target because their designs give them a demographic focus whether they like it or not. Let's contrast two sites to see how this works: The Pier (Figure 1) and CP Homes at Archer's Rock (Figure 2). The first is geared toward hip, twenty-something couples that are likely looking for their first home and are very interested in being a part of the city. The latter is focused in an equally obvious way, this one toward thirty-something families with small children. Perhaps the point of this is to remind designers working on real estate sites that they must carefully consider their target audience for the design they create because ultimately it will either connect with them and make sales easier, or it will alienate and drive them away. Regardless, this is a perfect set of examples to show how understanding your target audience can effectively control the end product. Real estate is obviously about sales, so anything that detracts from that should be removed. In both of these cases, the sites are so focused on their niche that it becomes a great first line of communication: Potential customers going to see a property after viewing these sites will have positive assumptions in place. This is a powerful tool for any salesperson.

Another site that also appeals to its target audience but is not consumer-driven is the Province West site (Figure 3). Because this site is geared toward professionals and financially-oriented people, it is a fantastic contrast to the consumer-driven examples discussed above. Here, we find simple navigation, a refined style that reeks of strength and stability, and a color palette that connects with a more conservative audience.

Figure 1 http://www.lifesabounce.com

Figure 2 http://www.cphomesatarchersrock.com

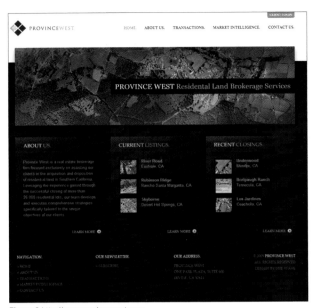

Figure 3 http://www.provincewest.com

http://www.championllc.com

http://www.bornliving.com

http://breedenhomes.com

http://www.hillwoodresidential.com

http://www.chrisfenemore.com

http://www.jprealtyservices.com

http://www.mpwproperties.com

http://www.alghadeer.ae

03 **sites by type**
iphone application • freelance • band • blog • personal • design firm • event • travel and tourism • e-commerce •
business card • web utility • web software • real estate • **portfolios** • coming soon • t-shirt • directory

portfolios

It seems that for every positive aspect a portfolio site might offer, there comes a downside on the same point. For example, portfolios can be bleeding-edge examples of what the future of the web has in store. On the downside, they can be an outright pain when they are experimental. As designers, we all require them and they serve to sell us day and night to anyone who is interested—and at the same time, they can miscommunicate our skills or typecast us when not thoroughly thought out.

Of all the types of sites in this book, this was by far the most common and the most difficult to select examples for. Gone are the days of the convoluted Flash portfolio (except for those who work in niches where this is actually appropriate). The

sites I included here share a refined directness that makes them more to the point.

Brian Hoff's portfolio (Figure 1) is a fantastic example of how refined and focused such a site can be. His core skills are highlighted up front with bold text stating he is a graphic designer (quickly avoiding the "What do you do?" question). While many portfolios jump straight to the work, this one focuses on him as a person, yet also allows for quick access to his portfolio.

Mark Dearman (Figure 2) has made use of my favorite approach to the straight portfolio site and put the work large and up front. There's no need for a lot of fuss, as his work is outstanding and needs little support. Often it seems that the skill level of a person is inversely related to the lengths to which they go to "dress up"

their portfolio. Mark's portfolio is simple yet elegantly designed, and it totally cuts to the chase.

And to demonstrate the opposite extreme of portfolio design I present the personal site of Ruy Adorno (Figure 3). Normally I am not a huge fan of Flash portfolios, especially when they contain gimmicky navigation. This site, however, made the cut for the book as I realized that it drew me in and had me playing with it. Let's face it, causing someone to play with your site and, therefore, get exposed to your work is a good thing—especially considering that this is the portfolio of a Flash developer who would like to do such work. So, in this case, the portfolio style matches the target and yet retains a simplicity that keeps it usable.

Figure 1 http://www.brianhoff.net

Figure 2 http://www.markdearman.com

http://www.dosbros.nl

Figure 3 http://www.ruyadorno.com

http://www.toby-powell.co.uk

I am constantly on the lookout for tools to do things faster. As a creative, there is no doubt that you can make a slick portfolio site, but there is seldom the time to do so. Enter the handy online portfolio creator. In recent years, several options have emerged that offer the ability to quickly create absolutely beautiful online portfolios. For some of you, your work is so amazing that this will more than do; for others, this will get you something up quickly while you work on that obnoxious Flash-based design!

My favorite portfolio builders are The Behance Network (behance.net), even though it is invitation only; the ever simple carbonmade.com site; and the newer krop.com hosted portfolio tool. All of these not only let you build a portfolio, but also help you spread your name.

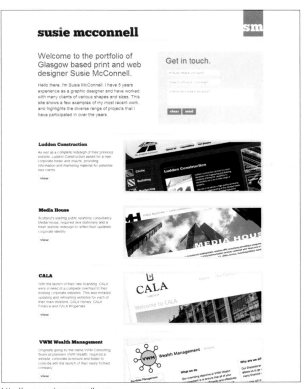

http://www.susiemcconnell.com

http://www.pyttel.sk

http://two24studios.com

http://www.yodabaz.com

http://www.shadddales.com

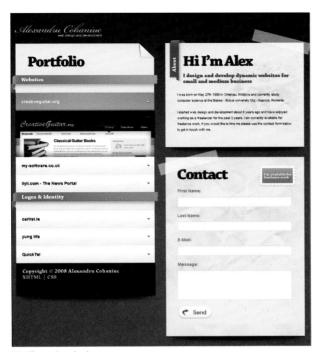

http://www.alexcohaniuc.com

http://sjhunter.net

http://www.ermanerkur.com

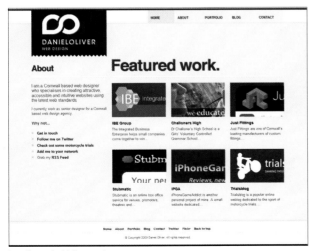

http://www.danieloliver.co.uk

03 / sites by type

iphone application • freelance • band • blog • personal • design firm • event • travel and tourism • e-commerce •
business card • web utility • web software • real estate • portfolios • **coming soon** • t-shirt • directory

coming soon

The coming soon page is certainly not a recent innovation, but gone are the days of a flashing construction sign that kindly informs you that what you are in search of might exist there someday—but it's up to you to find out if it ever does. It was almost like you were being taunted with the possibility. On the modern web, however, the coming soon page is put to work: If you manage to get someone to land on your site or page that isn't ready yet, you should do everything you can to capitalize on it.

One of the most basic things found on nearly every coming soon page is an e-mail sign-up form. There could not be a more highly focused marketing opportunity. If people land on this page and want to know when it is there, you know exactly what they are looking for and you can safely contact them once it launches. This can provide a real boost to a launch campaign when a new site goes live.

Some sites take a different approach; while they might not have everything the user might want, they can offer at least one critical element. The Designgraphy site (Figure 1) is a perfect example of this. The site might not be ready to go, but at least in this case a means of contacting the site owners keeps traffic from being fruitless.

Another popular tactic, found on Luke Beard's web site (Figure 2), is to direct the user to other means of connecting with the site's owner. In this case, the user is pointed to Luke's various social networks. It is likely he doesn't want to send out an e-mail campaign, so a sign-up form is not the best approach. But instead of losing the potential of any traffic, he directs them to other helpful alternatives.

For those of you wanting to invest more time and energy into such a landing page, SolidShops (Figure 3) offers an example of a more robust option. Here,

the coming soon site is nearly a full-blown site.

http://www.firenetworks.com

http://www.fireexchange.com

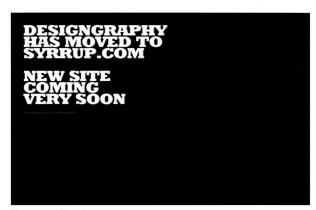

Figure 1 http://www.syrrup.com

Figure 2 http://www.lukesbeard.com

Figure 3 http://www.solidshops.com

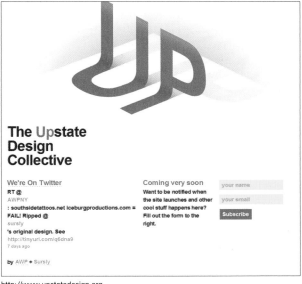

http://www.upstatedesign.org

notes from a developer

I know how hard it can be to invest the time it takes to create a good coming soon page with e-mail sign-up forms and all the bells and whistles. It's so much more tempting to delve into the project at hand. So, if you're a designer or marketer trying to wrangle your developer into putting up a slick coming soon page, one of the best things you can do is come to him with a resource to expedite the process.

For example, there are a variety of options for coming soon pages based on WordPress. Some of my favorites are from CSSJockey (http://wordpress.org/extend/plugins/custom-coming-soon-page/) and Launchpad (http://theme-shaper.com/wordpress-domain-parking-theme/). These out-of-the-box solutions will help you get what you're looking for with a very small amount of time from your developer. My recommendation would be to design around one of these pre-built themes.

http://www.branchesdesign.co.uk

http://www.freshdeals.com

http://www.shortinc.com

http://birdboxx.com

http://squidchef.com

http://wordpress-workshops.com

http://www.formmule.com

sites by type

iphone application • freelance • band • blog • personal • design firm • event • travel and tourism • e-commerce • business card • web utility • web software • real estate • portfolios • coming soon • **t-shirt** • directory

t-shirt

This is perhaps one of my favorite kinds of sites to browse as I, like many, am addicted to T-shirts. With such wide popularity, I have intentionally avoided including the obvious sites, like Threadless and Woot, for this section's examples; instead, I prefer to look at more fringe examples that bring different perspectives to this popular niche. So, if you're thinking about starting a site to sell your cotton works of art, here are some examples to chew on.

One of my favorites is Yellow Bird Project (Figure 1). The idea behind the site is totally unique and puts a great spin on the standard T-shirt site. Here, the shirts are all designed by indie rock artists, so you can get a shirt designed by fantastic bands. An idea such as this cannot carry a site all on its own (not usually, anyway), so we find a totally fresh and indie-styled site to match. Being an e-commerce site, the

level of creativity woven into this design is not to be second-guessed. It takes a lot of work to get an e-commerce site skinned with your typical clean design. In this case, the rough edges and hand-rendered items make for an extra layer of complexity in terms of implementation. Overall, this site functions as a standard e-commerce site, but has some fresh and niche-specific design elements that make it a joy to browse through and purchase from.

Unreal Cotton (Figure 2) is another great site to look at for inspiration. This site is fairly minimalistic and super clean. It gets to the point and is easy to browse and understand. Overall, the designers have gone to great lengths to make it as streamlined as possible. E-commerce systems are typically bloated and confusing since there are so many options to cover and features to offer; this often

means you end up with a site that is more complex than necessary. This site's focus and ease of use makes it a great sample of how things can be done. For example, the three tabs across the top let the user instantly drill down to the product line she is in search of. Such ease of use leads the user on a faster path to conversion, which is precisely what the site's owners want.

http://www.wuwi.com

Figure 1 http://www.yellowbirdproject.com

Figure 2 http://www.unrealcotton.com

http://www.cosmicsoda.com

http://www.milkandeggsco.com

http://www.ittybittee.com

https://www.drippinginfat.com

http://www.gotmojo.co.uk

http://www.riptapparel.com

http://200nipples.com

sites by type

iphone application • freelance • band • blog • personal • design firm • event • travel and tourism • e-commerce • business card • web utility • web software • real estate • portfolios • coming soon • t-shirt • **directory**

directory

The directory-style site is one that seldom gets much fanfare. Many of them are very spam-ish and seem to be there just to get some click-throughs. But then a shop submitted a series of directory sites they had built, and I knew I had something worth including in this book. These sites not only look nice, but they actually seem to be user-centric. The more I dug into them, the more I realized they took this niche to a new level.

Although most of us won't likely have a need to create directories, we can still learn a lot from these sites. For one, their goal is to make immense amounts of information approachable. When you land on the homepage for one of these sites, they have no idea what you're looking for. As such, they are great examples of how to help people get to what they are in search of as quickly as possible.

The Store Envy (Figure 1) is a great example to examine. On the surface, it is pretty clear, but when you consider the massive amount of data they have to work with, it is pretty amazing that the site feels approachable. In this case, they win by having you mill around until you find something you like. From there, you can easily click through to similar items. It has a browsing type of experience that lends itself to random discovery. Other sites are more mechanical than this, but ultimately the lessons are the same. They demonstrate ways of organizing massive amounts of data.

http://www.patriciaferreira.com

Figure 1 http://www.storenvy.com

http://www.aroundme.com

http://www.theuxbookmark.com

http://www.practicelink.com

http://www.freshdeals.com

04/

sites by design elements

Design elements come in a wide array of shapes, sizes, and styles. Some reflect mostly trendy design while others are the result of necessity. What fascinates me about these groupings though is that each and every one of them has a purpose. For as much as each of these has a way of being used that gives it a clear and intentional purpose, they can just as easily reflect a total lack of intention (clearly we will focus on the former). My deepest hope on this topic is that designers won't look on these chapters as design clichés to abuse, but rather as functional tools to be leveraged at the appropriate time. All I ask is that you endeavor to use these elements wisely and with purpose; this only requires a little thought, and that will carry you a long way. Think before you design and you will always find that the end product is better for it.

the pitch

While this is not a book on marketing, the topic of giving a pitch almost inevitably comes up. An elevator pitch is a sales pitch that can be given quickly (as in the length of a short elevator ride). Samples of incredibly short ones might be "I am a web designer" or "We build houses." In this chapter is a set of sites that employ a prominent elevator pitch, most commonly on their homepage.

This design element plays a crucial role in rapidly communicating to a user. Visitors to a web site often have an incredibly short attention span and an insatiable thrust for efficiency. Though most users might not describe it as efficiency, this is exactly what is happening. Consider just how helpful it is to immediately understand the purpose of the organization behind a web site. In fact, their very ability to sum up exactly what they do best

is a sure sign of a focused and polished organization. Let's look at some samples to see how this might work.

On the Concept Feedback site (Figure 1), the sales pitch "Free feedback for marketers and designers" is critical to helping users know why they are here and why they should stay. We immediately know whom this site is for, and the free part removes the most common barrier to entry: money.

One of my favorite examples of a homepage pitch is on the personal site for Andrew Barden (Figure 2). He simply states: "Hello. I like to design things." While this leaves it vague enough to allow him to work in multiple mediums, it is succinct enough that we don't wonder if he is a developer, a shop full of a hundred people, or some sort of submarine parts company. It cuts to the chase and not

only lets you know why you're here, but it lets you know in a way that invites you in further.

While the pitch statement on the Kindred Spirits site (Figure 3) is a bit longer, and perhaps less likely to be read, its prominent placement and large type at least gives it a reasonable chance of being read. In this case, the message comes across more like a mission statement than a quick summary, and I must say I agree with the decision as it would be very difficult to sum up the concept in fewer words.

Ultimately, this is a tool that can be invaluable in rapidly communicating a purpose. Careful consideration of the clarity of the message and the design in which it is presented will ensure that it works as expected.

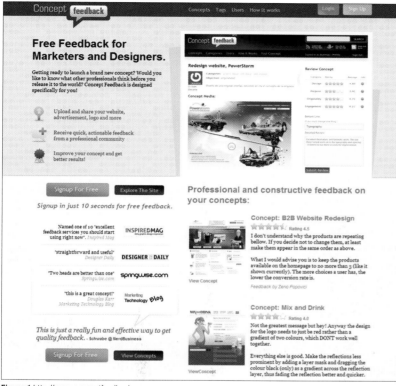

Figure 1 http://www.conceptfeedback.com

http://www.patrickmonkel.nl

Figure 2 http://www.periscopecreative.com

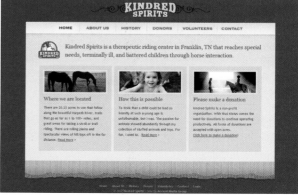

Figure 3 http://kindredspiritstn.org

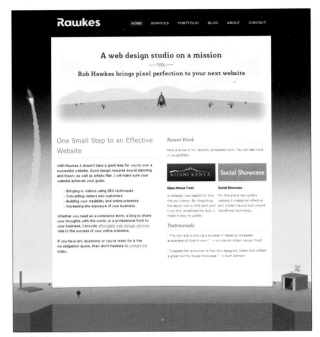

http://rawkes.com

http://www.performanceedgepartners.com

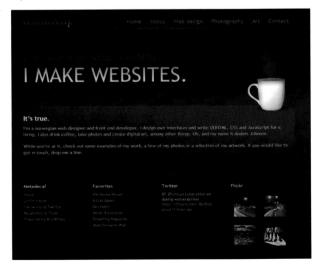

http://www.antidecaf.com

http://www.smalldotstudios.com

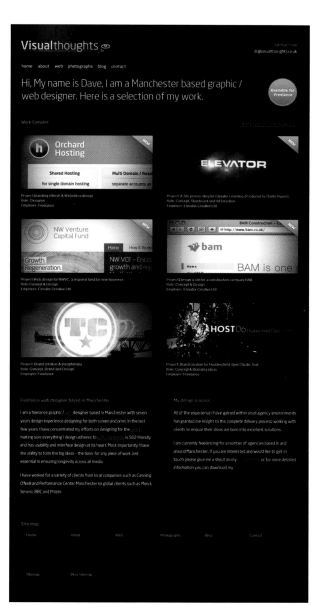

http://www.design-manchester.co.uk

http://www.arcticcat.com/snow

http://www.studiow.com.my

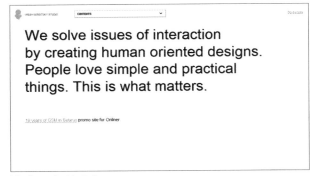

http://www.skrotskystudio.com

> We solve issues of interaction by creating human oriented designs. People love simple and practical things. This is what matters.

http://wtmworldwide.com

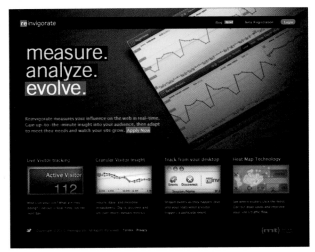

http://www.reinvigorate.net

lighting

Lighting and illumination in web design can be a powerful design tool. The first thing to realize if you are new to this style is that it almost never uses the stereotypical lighting imagery—there are no light bulbs or hanging light fixtures in these designs. Rather, we find that the designs have been imbued with a sense of internal illumination that creates a certain aesthetic and atmosphere. Let's look at some specific sites to see what has been accomplished with this subtle element.

The Strutta site (Figure 1) is a prime example of how illumination can be leveraged. It is quite likely that the designer didn't necessarily consider this a lighting technique; instead, it was probably seen as an extension of a refined glossy style.

Regardless, the end result is something that gives the sense of internal illumination. In this case, the style has been used not only to reflect an overall design style, but to draw focus to a key element of the page. The intro video that gives the quick overview is a key conversion tool that is brought to the forefront by the contrast of the illuminated backgrounds.

Another subtle demonstration of this style is found on the Pizza Inn site (Figure 2). Here, a radial burst accents the gradient background. Again, I doubt the designer intended to illuminate the scene, and yet this is just what has been done. The lighting makes the content pop and gives the page depth and a rich visual interest.

http://ryanmcmaster.com

Figure 1 http://strutta.com

Figure 2 http://www.pizzainn.com

http://www.zionseven.net

http://trystentertainment.com

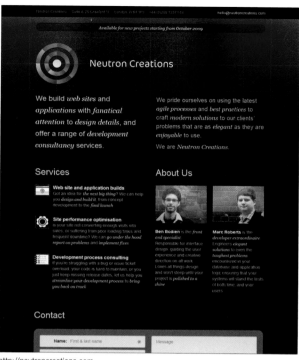

http://neutroncreations.com

http://tomatogallery.yzx.se

http://www.digitalgurus.co.uk

http://www.addnoise.nl

http://www.mdxinteractive.com

notes from a developer

While this style will not likely have a serious impact on implementation costs, there are some instances where it can be a bit of a pain. If your lighting technique relies on outer glows and lots of gradients, it is likely to cause some trouble.

Outer glows in particular are notorious for driving developers crazy. This is especially true when these items have roll-over states or otherwise have to change based on a user's action. Carefully consider how glow effects might interact with the elements around them (at least when it is an element the user will interact with). For example, a button with an outer glow over a gradient background will mean one of two things: either the image will be partially transparent (and require some PNG hacking to get working), or it will have to contain the background image as part of it, and will therefore be subject to very precise positioning needs.

In the end, this isn't a showstopper—it's just important to realize that gradients, drop shadows and outer glows can be elements that require careful attention to avoid problems.

http://www.factoria.me

http://cannonballcommunications.com

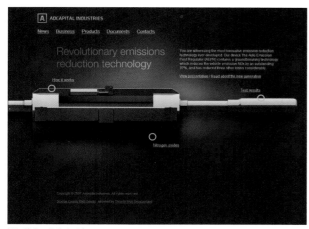

http://adcapitalindustries.com

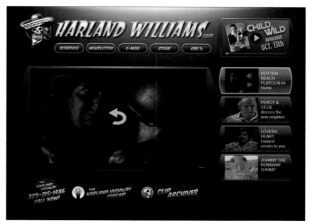

http://www.harlandwilliams.com

http://kissmetrics.com

iphone as flourish

There are three things that make the iPhone a popular design flourish that has worked its way into countless web sites. First and foremost, the device is just beautiful; it makes my old flip phone look like an antiquated piece of junk. Secondly, the iPhone is massively popular and very current. So, in a small way, sites that leverage it in their designs are perhaps trying to say they are current or hip. Finally, many sites have iPhone-specific content, and displaying the gorgeous device is a sure-fire way to communicate this.

The Gelattina site (Figure 1) is a perfect example of this design element. In this case, it could easily be argued that the iPhone in the design is not necessary because it serves a more decorative role. But as it stands, the device fits in nicely with the desktop collage style and is a clever way to show a video.

Arat (Figure 2) is a development shop that focuses on Mac and iPhone development, so it is no surprise to find a large image of an iPhone on their homepage. What struck me as interesting about this site's design was that it puts a reflection beneath the device, which actually does something slightly remarkable. This simple reflection roots the device in the real world and reminds us that it is a real, three-dimensional thing. This, combined with the overlap of the border with the header, creates an illusion of subtle depth.

Figure 1 http://www.gelattina.com

Figure 2 http://arat.cz

http://www.bottlerocketapps.com

http://www.cellar-app.com

notes from a developer

The implementation of this style really depends on how it is used. If the element is simply a part of the visuals and doesn't function or interact with the user, then it's a no-brainer. On the other hand, if you want it to be an interactive element, to behave at all like a real iPhone or to have it play a video, there will be a cost implication.

If you want to play a movie, load it up in Flash and embed it in the page on top of the image of the device. No big deal.

For a more interactive version, the Yahoo! design library offers some great stencil sets, one of which contains iPhone assets perfect for working into a design. Download the set for free here: http://developer.yahoo.com/ypatterns/about/stencils.

http://icedcocoa.com

http://www.imagemakers.uk.com

http://www.liftux.com

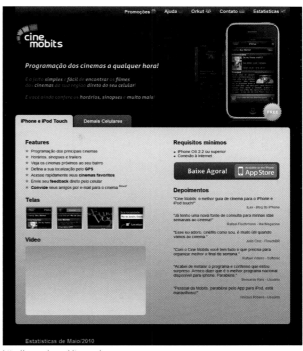

Estatisticas de Maio/2010

http://www.cinemobits.com.br

http://www.magnateinteractive.com

http://www.mockdraftapp.com

http://www.flipside5.com

http://www.rovingbird.com/touringmobilis-nl

social media links

It is not the least bit surprising to find that links to various social media sites show up all over web sites. From corporate sites to personal blogs, links to Twitter, Facebook and other social platforms abound. There are loads of free icon sets for this purpose, and what I looked at in these examples is how the social media icon links have been worked into the design.

One of the most common approaches is to place all of the links in a list at the bottom of the page, as seen on the sites for Kim Burgess (Figure 1) and Lisa Bun (Figure 2). This convenient location has become very popular and is found in the footer of many sites. It makes good sense, too. Once you have consumed the site's content, you are presented with some links to other places to connect to the site or its owner.

Another tactic for icon location is prominent placement at the top of a page, as seen on the site for Aus120 (Figure 3). Here, we find the links at the top right corner, one of the most prominent locations on the site. For this site and others that choose this placement for links, building a following on social networks is a top priority. The same thing is found on Michael Austin's site (Figure 4). Though in this case, the icons are even more prominent, and a large Twitter feed is displayed at the top as well.

In other sites, like John Philips's mini site (Figure 5), we see that social media links have become the primary purpose of the site, and the homepage is nothing more than a portal to the various networks John participates in.

As with many design elements (or content elements, in this case), designers often forget to consider the goals of a site. The placement, prominence and design of these social media links should be driven by the site's goals.

http://www.albertlo.com

Figure 1 http://www.kimburgess.info

Figure 2 http://www.lisabun.com

Figure 4 http://maustingraphics.com

Figure 3 http://www.aus120.com

notes from a developer

Social media is all the rage, so it is not surprising that the logos and links to these platforms have become a common part of web design. The technicalities of implementing these are very little, if any, and really have no impact on the end cost of a project.

While implementing simple links might be no big deal, showing a live feed of activity from these social platforms is not quite as easy. Showing RSS feeds is not too much work, but if you want to show live data from a third party, you're likely to have a few complications to get around. This will typically involve issues with calling the web service and handling contingencies like a service being unavailable.

Some of my favorite (and free) social media icon sets include:

- **The extensive Komodo Media set:**
  http://www.komodomedia.com/blog/2009/06/social-network-icon-pack

- **Vikiworks's round social network icons:**
  http://vikiworks.com/2007/07/28/social-bookmark-iconset-part-2

- **Jankoatwarpspeed.com's sketchy style icons:**
  http://www.jankoatwarpspeed.com/post/2008/10/20/Handycons-a-free-hand-drawn-social-media-icon-set.aspx and http://www.jankoatwarpspeed.com/post/2009/02/23/Handycons-2-another-free-hand-drawn-icon-set.aspx

http://adellecharles.com

http://www.cucweb.org

Figure 5 http://www.johnphillips.me

http://www.visualgroove.net

http://www.kmkzband.com

http://3diddi.com

http://www.levikoi.com

icons

The icon is to the web what hood ornaments are to the car (or at least what they were in the 1970s). Icons can communicate so much information in so little space, they cry out to be used. As such, icons have been used in almost every way imaginable. I've picked out some of the more interesting samples to illustrate how to leverage their quick communicating power.

One of my favorites is the 53 Mondays site (Figure 1). In this case, hand-rendered icons break the standard pixel-perfect model and mesh with the site perfectly. They may be a free library, but you wouldn't know since the icons fit in so well. It would appear that the icons fit so well that they must have been hand created for this design. They still call on common themes in terms of what is depicted in the icons, which is how they become so functional. They rely on the standard imagery, but are presented in a totally fresh way.

Sometimes it is good to remember that icons don't have to dictate the entire direction of a design, and that they can be more effective as simple supporting elements. The Grooveshark VIP site proves this point perfectly (Figure 2). In this case, the icons are only in the bottom part of the site, but they still serve a communication role. This region of the design is more dense with content, and the icons help break it up and allow for quick scanning to find the content you're in need of.

Let's compare that site to the portfolio site of Lieve Sonke (Figure 3). Here, the icons basically are the design—they are larger than normal and sit on little ledges like trophies waiting to be viewed. The icons barely need defining, and the supporting text for each is pretty small. These function really well, as the icons call on their most well-known meanings.

Figure 1 http://53mondays.com

Figure 2 http://vip.grooveshark.com

http://www.thepeachdesign.com

Figure 3 http://www.id83.nl

http://theiconlab.com

From a developer's standpoint, the icon doesn't present many problems during implementation. So instead, I will point out a few key assets that can really help you find the right direction (assuming you're looking for a stock icon set).

Iconfinder.net is a fantastic search tool that will help you find many options for any basic icon needs. Once you get a sense of direction for your site's design, use this to see if you can find an entire set to fit your needs.

If you're designing for an application, one of the most popular sets to use is one from famfamfam.com. It's a huge set (more than 700 icons), and best of all, it's free.

Sometimes following standards is a helpful thing as you can draw on industry norms; standardized RSS feed icons can be found at feedicons.com.

Also, check the section in this book on social media links on page 119 for pointers to some other nice icon sets in that niche.

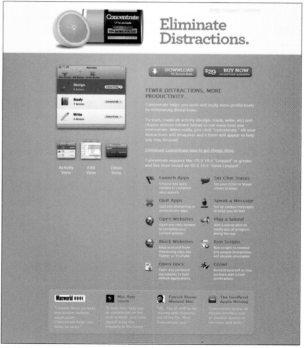

http://getconcentrating.com

http://www.gositewave.com

http://www.ebandlive.com

http://www.jp3design.com

http://nmiciano.com

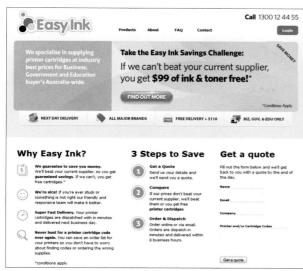

http://www.easyink.com.au

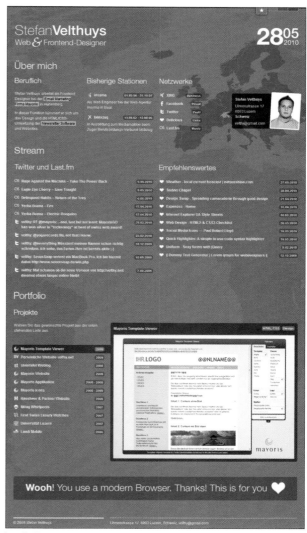

http://velthy.net

http://www.southernmedia.net

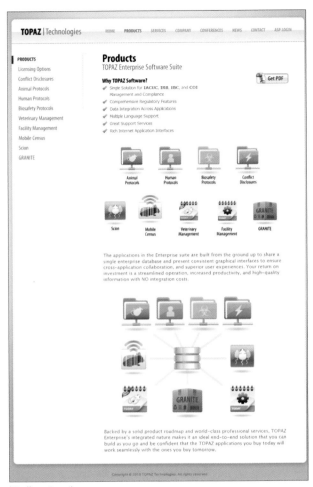

http://www.topazti.com

http://www.shape5.com

typographic

Typography on the web has always been limited, at times neglected, and most often scowled at by designers wanting to implement their typographic masterpieces. Their beautiful designs are often created in Photoshop, and the harsh realities of how web sites are made squash the ambitions of the otherwise hopeful designer. However, there are many tools in place that allow creatives' work to be replicated very effectively, especially when designers more fully understand the limitations they are operating under.

The limits of web site typography are often a bitter pill to swallow, but the examples provided here prove that beauty can prevail. One of my favorite examples is Darren Hoyt's personal site (Figure 1). Beautifully designed titles rule the site and define its style. These lovely titles eliminate the need for supporting graphics and are the singular element that elevates this otherwise simple design to a higher level. Sure, all the other details need to be in place, but the typographic treatment ensures a beautiful design.

The coDesign site (Figure 2) is a fantastic example of a designer working comfortably around the limitations of the web. No special tricks have been employed to make use of fonts that aren't web-safe. Instead, the designer embraced the safe fonts and simply made the design work with them. This makes for a lean site (code wise) and should have helped reduce the development time (and, thereby, the maintenance costs). Designs like this remind me how important it is for creatives to jump in and code something. Once you see the limitations, it is much easier to create a design that plays nice.

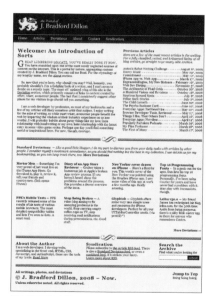

http://jbradforddillon.com

Figure 1 http://www.darrenhoyt.com

Figure 2 http://thecodesign.org

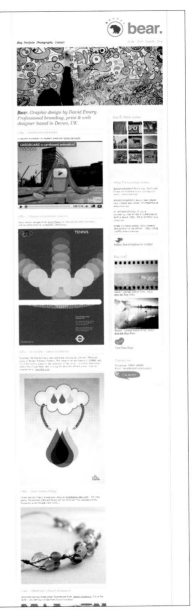

http://beargraphics.co.uk

http://www.behoff.com

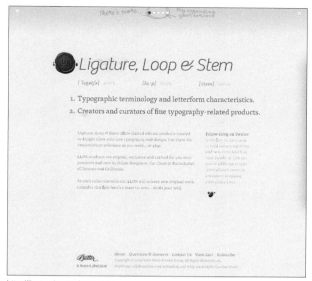

http://ligatureloopandstem.com

notes from a developer

For designers new to the web, the typography limitations can be painful. Short of creating lots and lots of images for headings, there are actually some practical solutions that are pretty easy to implement.

Three solid solutions to rendering fonts outside the web-safe list are sIFR (http://www.mikeindustries.com/blog/sifr), cufón (http://cufon.shoqolate.com/generate/) and Typekit (http://typekit.com/). The first two are free, and the last is commercial. I have used sIFR on numerous sites, and it's pretty simple to implement. Once set up, it renders text in the desired typeface dynamically, making it hands off once it's installed.

The real complication comes when using these tools with backgrounds that are not a solid color. This is something to pay attention to and to work closely with your developer on to ensure your design can be implemented and easily maintained. After all, the real question isn't if you can use a typeface, but rather, how much it will cost to maintain and work with. Automated solutions such as these will keep the cost low and the aesthetics high.

http://www.typechart.com

http://www.thevileplutocrat.com

http://www.integritystl.com

http://www.piscataqua.com/index.aspx

http://www.squarefour.net

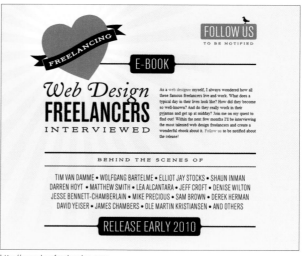

http://www.lovefreelancing.com

http://malwin-faber.de

http://www.votedougducey.com

photographic backgrounds

The use of photographs or otherwise complex backgrounds over solid colors, patterns and simple gradients has been popular in web design for a long time. From a designer's perspective, it offers a unique situation and some interesting possibilities in terms of the design.

Traditionally, many sites make use of this style in a beautiful yet basic way. For example, the sites for Leaf Tea Shop & Bar (Figure 1) and The Creative Dot (Figure 2) have complex backgrounds that lead to inevitably simpler foregrounds. The image sets the mood of the site and communicates something about the site's purpose. While this design is effective, it seems that many have begun pushing the style a bit further.

What gets really interesting is when the background image actually becomes a part of the content. On Rommil Santiago's site (Figure 3)], for example, the flower is in the background, and yet it's part of the foreground. The space left in the foreground actually makes the flower move forward, but it is overlapped by the foremost items. So it somehow lives halfway between.

We see this again on Noah Shrader's site (Figure 4). The background image is equally a part of the content itself. This dynamic makes the background an even more functional part of the site. Overall, it helps make the site distinct and unique, but also enables a sort of minimalism that leads to streamlined communication and a clear flow in the content.

It's exciting to find niche web design tools like the photographic background that are being leveraged in fresh ways. I am sure this has been done before, but it is an approach worth talking about and shows how something simple can be put to work in a complex and effective way. It makes me want to reconsider many basic elements that get put into my designs without extensive thought.

http://www.bensky.co.uk

Figure 1 http://www.thisisleaf.co.uk

http://www.housetopmedia.com

http://blog.newsok.com/afghanistan-iraq/mikes-blog

Figure 2 http://www.njwebdesign.co.za

Figure 3 http://www.rommil.com

Figure 4 http://www.noahshrader.com

http://www.davyknowles.com

If your design relies on portions of the background image showing through into content regions of the site, you're likely to hear your developer complain about this. If items over the background need to be able to move, transparent PNGs are inevitable. If the items don't need to move, the transparency can often be simulated by placing images appropriately.

PNGs are a file format similar to JPEG and GIF, except that they allow for alpha transparency. This means they can have varying degrees of transparency, much like items in Photoshop. This does cause some browser issues and will require a fix for good old Internet Explorer. One of the best solutions can be found here: http://www.twinhelix.com/css/iepngfix. All in all, this should not be a showstopper, but your developer will have to put a work-around into place. Overall, the cost implication should be minimal.

http://www.albus.fi

137

http://www.superieur-graphique.com

http://www.dettaglio.co.uk

http://v1.maykelloomans.com

http://www.lightqube.co.uk

http://www.schlossanger.de

05/

ultra clean • minimal • sketchy • collage • illustrated •
type-focused • solid colors • fabric • wood

sites by styles and themes

One might think that styles and themes are one and the same (if only because I group them together here), but in fact, they each have their own—but similar—purpose. It seems that styles represent more vague approaches to things that don't necessarily employ a particular visual element. For example while "retro design" is a style it doesn't dictate a particular imagery. All of this contrasts sharply with themes. A theme in and of itself dictates a particular visual vocabulary. For example, a sketchy theme will inevitable have some hand drawn elements in it. All this really means is that themes and styles are different ways of thinking about how you design a page. One could have a retro minimal style site or an illustrated ultra clean one. The idea here is to consider the basic approaches you can take to a design and figure out how to leverage them to your benefit.

ultra clean

If I had to pick a single style or approach to web design to use, it would have to be this one. The designs in this section represent for me not just a style, but an ideal in terms of clean and functional design. Ultra-clean sites lean toward minimalism, but they are not so focused on being less as they are on being crystal clear. As such, these sites are a joy to look at and are uniformly easy to use. They provide a great target to shoot for in terms of polish and functionality.

Let's start with the Nosotros web site (Figure 1) as an example of this style. The delicate touches throughout this design combined with an airy layout make this site sing. With an abstract name and a nondescript logo, the text on the homepage introduces the company and communicates a bit about how they approach design work. They set themselves apart from the stereotypes of agencies and support this by having a killer site. I can't imagine a more effective sales pitch. Sure, agencies have their place, but there is a market for the anti-agency (just as there is for freelancers or high school kids building web pages). The cleanliness of this site tells the user they can back up their words and lets you get hooked on them in an instant.

The NanoIntegris site demonstrates how powerful a clean site can be (Figure 2). In this otherwise dry manufacturing niche, the company showcases itself as a high-end company tuned in to the latest styles and technologies. This site makes learning about the company's products easy and clear, and it avoids the typical confusion found with extremely technical and complicated products.

http://www.brianhoff.net

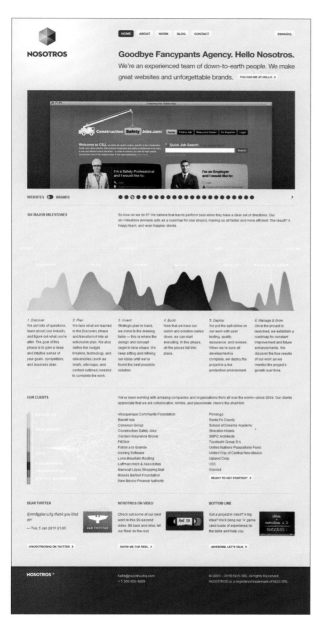

Figure 1 http://www.nosotroshq.com

Figure 2 http://www.nanointegris.com

http://eighty8four.com

http://www.jamiegregory.co.uk

http://fusionads.net

http://kiwithemes.com

http://nihongoup.com

http://www.rihardsonline.com

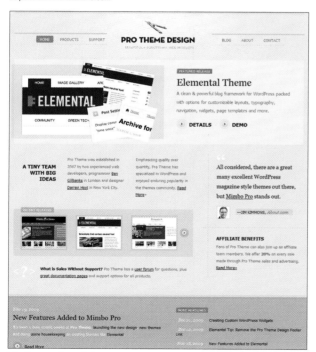

http://www.prothemedesign.com

http://www.hotgloo.com

http://www.admkids.com

http://www.paperrep.com

http://www.pixelflips.com

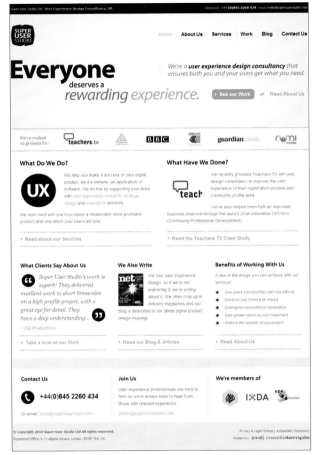

http://www.superuserstudio.com

minimal

The minimalist style has always been popular, and it seems to maintain its status as one of the most viable and well-received approaches to web design. Not only does this style potentially offer the most usable designs, it also tends to produce ones that are timeless. Sites in this style are also typically easier to build and maintain. Don't be deceived, though—the minimal style is not easy to design or to implement. It requires painstaking attention to detail, and a keen eye for the subtleties of design.

The Inbox Awards (Figure 1) web site is an interesting example of this style. Not only is it minimalist in nature, it also incorporates a very atypical layout and navigation system. As a site that showcases great design, a minimalist style makes perfect sense. The work being showcased

(instead of some fancy e-mail-based theme) is allowed to grab the full attention of the viewer. In this case, the style doesn't say much about the site's owners or the content directly, but it does reflect a pragmatic focus on the content and a desire to make it the showcase of the site.

The retrostrobe site (Figure 2) offers another fine version of this style and shows that just because the style is called minimal, it doesn't have to be lame, boring or otherwise uninteresting. Here, we see a design that functions to allow the user to get an insight into the approach this agency might take on a project. It would seem they look at a project and find the best, most efficient way to communicate the site's goals. In this case, a minimal style showcases the agency in a posi-

tive light as an effective, results-oriented shop. And we get all that from the style they selected. It is up to them to live up to that, but the message they communicate with their design is inevitable.

Another interesting minimalist example is the Sreski site (Figure 3). While it may be tempting to use a white background for a traditional minimal-style site, this example shows that you can still have a minimal style with a nonwhite/different colored/dark background. On this site, the trimmed-down design lets the work shine. What really strikes me about the design is how the image layout is adapted to fit the images. Why crop these long images to simple squares? Instead, the designer worked to show the pieces in the best possible way. It's truly refreshing.

Figure 1 http://www.inboxaward.com

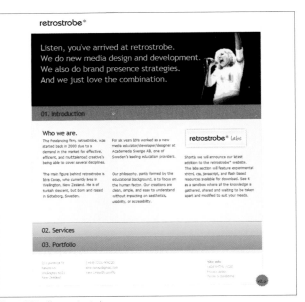

Figure 2 http://www.retrostrobe.com

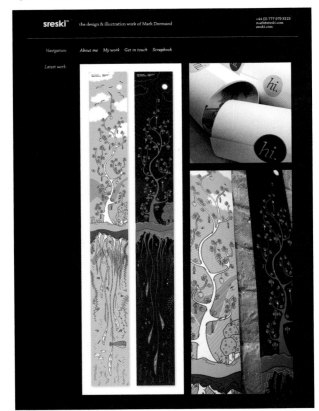

Figure 3 http://www.sreski.com

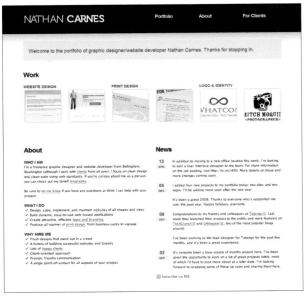

http://nathancarnes.com

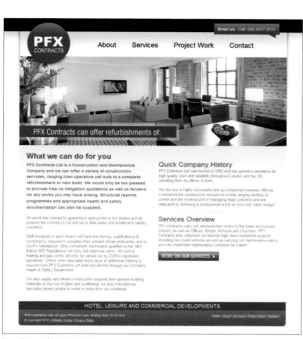

http://www.pfxcontracts.net

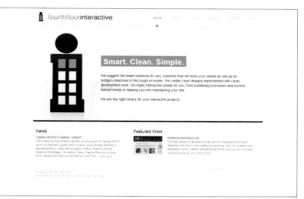

http://www.fourthfloorinteractive.com

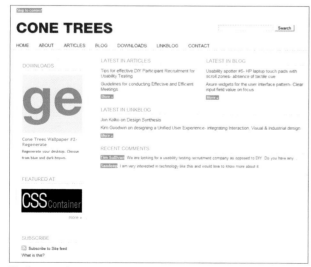

http://www.conetrees.com

http://robertsonuk.net

http://www.studiozfilms.com

http://www.ryanjclose.com

http://www.playout.pt

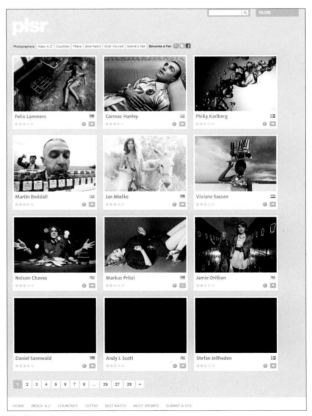

http://plsr.net

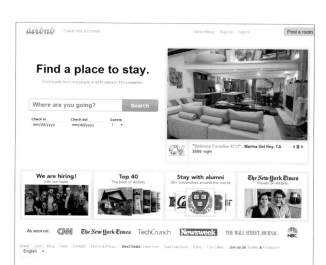

http://www.airbnb.com

http://www.diografic.com

http://lensco.be

http://www.rozner.pl

sketchy

One surefire way to create a totally unique design is to incorporate hand-drawn elements into it. This works for obvious reasons—no two people will draw the same thing in the same style with the same imagery. Even when two people set out to sketch the same object, they will approach it with different techniques, different compositions and different personal histories. As such, this style finds its way into a number of sites. Let's look at a few examples.

The sketchy style of the Twiggy site (Figure 1) comes across as totally unique; in no way does it feel the same as any other site. In this case, the style connects with an organic and hip atmosphere. It appears to be a project from Internet

hipsters instead of some uber-nerd code junkies. Who knows if this is true or not: In many ways, it doesn't matter. Ultimately, they are pushing a product, and the image they present is key.

In other cases, such as Camelia Dobrin's site (Figure 2), the purpose is far more literal and obvious. Here, it is the portfolio site of a creative. As such, it does the artist well to show off her skills. The simple drawing on the homepage is unique and portrays the individual's style very clearly. We see this approach on other sites, like that of Jessette Dayate (Figure 3). Again, the individual's unique style is clearly and prominently communicated with the site's hand-drawn visuals. These illustrations not only decorate the

page, they also communicate to the user what the site's owner does.

Another purpose of hand-drawn elements is to connect with the root purpose of a site. Such is the case with the Greenville site (Figure 4). Being an organization that operates in the health care industry, it faces some key challenges. Foremost is an impersonal stigma. This is most likely what drove them to a hand-drawn style for their site. Not only does it present them in a unique way (especially within the industry), it also attempts to let the consumer know that the company isn't lifeless. This personal style connects with the user in a way that breaks down some of the stereotypes and assumptions about what a health care experience will be.

Figure 1 http://twiggy.carsonified.com

Figure 2 http://www.camellie.com

Figure 4 http://www.happyingreenville.com

Figure 3 http://www.crayonslife.com

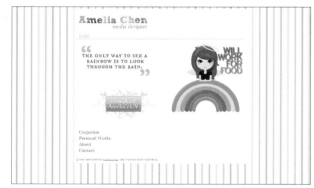

http://ami.wookypooky.com

notes from a developer

This is one of those styles that could be an implementation nightmare, or it might have no impact on things at all. It all depends on the design. Here are some important things to consider that will impact how much your developer wants to strangle you.

How many elements do you have that will have to be rendered in a custom way each time copy changes? (For example, a page header that has type rendered by hand.) This will get tiresome after a while, so it better be really necessary. Two great ways around this situation are handwriting fonts that can be combined with tools found in the Typography section of this book on page 129, or this nifty font generator that uses your own handwriting to make the file: http://www.yourfonts.com.

Another important thing to look for is overlaps and odd alignments. If your sketchy design includes elements that break borders and merge multiple items, it will cause a slight amount of extra work for your developer.

This style isn't likely to break the budget when used wisely.

http://www.rawcoach.be

http://www.tylergaw.com

http://mesonprojekt.com

http://www.albertocerriteno.com

http://www.chrisspooner.com

http://www.espiratecnologias.com

http://www.ebandlive.com/users/dirtydozenbrassband803

collage

The collage style is one that seems to never go out of style. This versatile style creates a design that brings in numerous design elements that all carry their own meaning. Together, they create a collage that not only looks visually interesting, but also contains many messages about the content and people behind a site. What's perhaps most interesting about the set of samples here is the extremely diverse range of topics the style shows up in.

For example, the Real Sangria (Figure 1) site uses the style to create a pattern-based focal point for the page, while the Adam's Magic site (Figure 2) creates a much more playful and fun style with the same technique. Both designs piece together various elements and draw on an aged and worn style, yet they communicate radically different messages. Perhaps this flexibility explains the appeal of the style.

Other sites put this approach to use for more aesthetic purposes. That is to say, there is less meaning in it and it's more about just looking sharp. Matt Northam's site (Figure 4) and the Duirwaigh Studios (Figure 3) site use the style to make the page feel fresh and unique. Yes, the collages on these sites create a very distinct style and set a certain mood, but overall it is more about creating something beautiful to look at.

One of the most common uses of the collage style is to create a retro atmosphere. This style easily connects with the early to mid-1900s and is a perfect solution to reference that time period in a stylish way. The Sign Shop site (Figure 5) is a prime example of this.

The collage style is one of the more overused design styles and seems to frequently be used when no other more thoughtful style is found. I suspect this style can be a crutch designers rely upon. So it is always refreshing to find good examples of it and consider how it can effectively be saved as a potential style in our design library.

Figure 1 http://real-sangria.com

Figure 3 http://www.Duirwaigh.com

Figure 2 http://www.adamsmagic.com

Figure 4 http://www.mattnortham.com

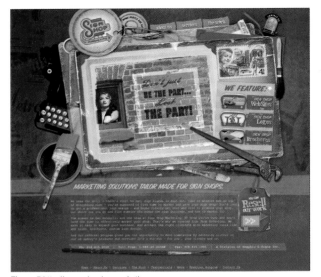

Figure 5 http://www.signshopmarketing.com

http://chirp.twitter.com

http://www.carbonsugar.com

http://www.bbc.co.uk/cbbc/tracybeaker

notes from a developer

The issues created by many collage styles will actually reflect problems found with transparent images, as noted in the Photographic Backgrounds section on page 135. Beyond that, the impact this style has on the developer depends on the design. If the collage regions are contained, it is likely to just be a static image. If, however, the collage is pervasive throughout the design and overlaps many borders, there will be some considerations. First, many developers will observe that collage elements crossing the borders of containers might be problematic, but a dash of CSS positioning tactics combined with some transparent PNGs should solve this problem. The real issue for the developer is more likely to be the visually demanding style this often creates. By this, I mean that this style often produces designs that are visually intertwined, making it very important for the developer to replicate the design perfectly. This level of precision will likely increase the cost of converting the design into functional code.

http://bigskynj.com

http://arose.biz

http://www.comfortbrothers.com

http://zionsnowboards.com

http://blog.spoongraphics.co.uk

http://www.joaozanatta.com.br

http://www.swimmingwithbabies.com

illustrated

As a designer, it is not uncommon to find that a gift for illustration can come in handy. Perhaps the most distinct advantage this offers is the ability to add something fresh and unique to the design. And in a digital world where attention spans are nonexistent, anything to stand out is openly welcomed.

Let's look at a site developed by my friends at FireHost (Figure 1). Web hosting isn't exactly cool, and it wouldn't be much of a stretch to put it in the nerdy bucket. That being said, this site's fresh design brings a great personification of hosting, servers, security, hackers and the like to the table. The comic book style illustrations and animation bring life to this design and make it stand out. The overall design flows well with the comic book characters, but the designer didn't overdo it and put everything in speech bubbles

or a half-tone pattern. For me, this strikes the perfect balance of thematic and traditional design.

On the Lionite site (Figure 2), we find an illustrated style where the theme has been carried to every aspect of the design. What saves the design from being carried too far is an illustration style that is not loud and obnoxious, but rather subdued, clean and orderly. In this case, the style reflects the personality of the people behind the site and helps the visitor see them as humans and not just another stock photo of some lady on the phone pretending to be helpful.

A few of the sites from Saizen Media Studios (Figures 3, 4 and 5) demonstrate how a web site can truly be a work of art. This style is probably not possible for the bulk of us, but this is not to say that we can't be inspired by it. The goal here is

to break the conceptions that keep us designers from seeing such approaches as a viable option.

http://www.francescomugnai.com

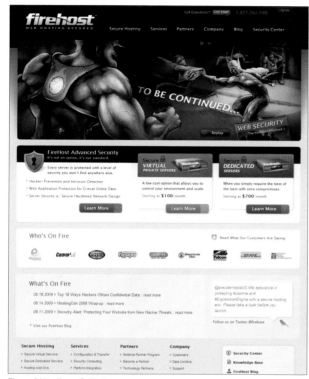

Figure 1 http://www.firehost.com

Figure 2 http://www.lionite.com

http://www.edelwwwweiss.com

http://www.launchmind.com

Figure 3 http://www.emergence-day.com

http://kiwi-app.net

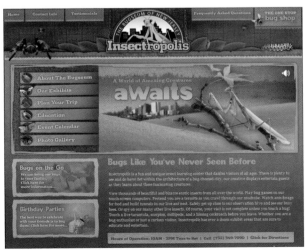

http://insectropolis.com

Figure 4 http://www.saizenmedia.com/FFIV

Figure 5 http://www.saizenmedia.com/nightwish

http://www.cupcakecarousel.co.uk

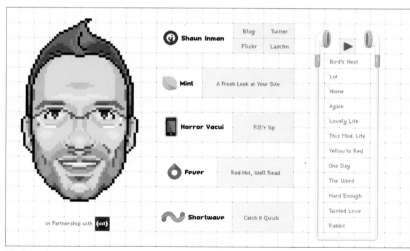

http://shauninman.com

http://culturapositiva.com

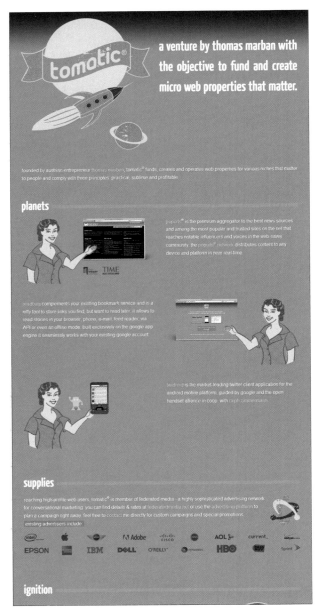

http://tomatic.com

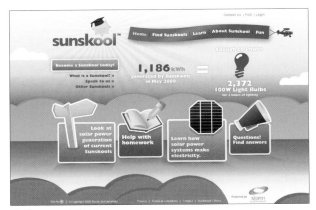

http://www.sunskool.com

http://events.carsonified.com

http://www.mikimottes.com

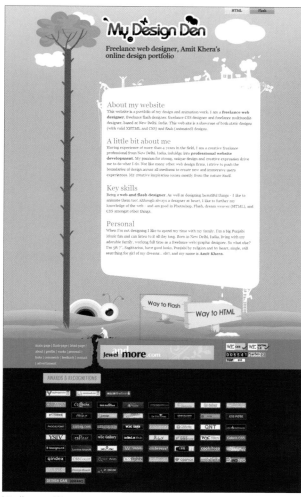

http://www.amitkhera.com

http://www.2pitch.com

type-focused

In this section, we will focus on designs that leverage type as the predominant element. Most of these designs could easily be considered minimalist, and perhaps this is just a different way of looking at the same topic. The slight difference here is that the focus is on the usage of type in elegant ways.

On the portfolio and personal site of Shay Howe (Figure 1), for example, the design is by all means minimalist, makes use of solid colors and lines to differentiate content, and uses type as an element of design. In particular, the basic type-driven logo sets the mood for the entire design. Huge benefits of such an approach are fast-loading pages and content that is extremely easy to consume.

Another of my favorite examples of type-focused design is the Johny Favourite site (Figure 2). Here, the type is treated in an elegant and beautiful way; the simple contrast of color combined with such a clear hierarchy in the page makes this mini site crystal clear. The irony of an example like this is that it looks so easy, yet delicately manipulating type to look this great takes a lot of work.

One surprising place to find such an approach is on a site for a design shop, like the Buckenmeyer & Co. homepage (Figure 3). It's surprising because most creative shops can't resist the temptation to put their creative juices to work and generate a highly visual design. Instead, this minimalist, type-focused design presents the content with a totally different atmosphere. The site comes across as bold and confident, yet conservative and reliable. It's strange how so much can be inferred from the style of design selected.

http://www.endemit.si

Figure 1 http://www.shayhowe.com

Figure 2 http://dj.johnyfavourite.co.uk

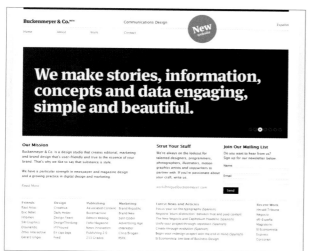

Figure 3 http://www.miguelbuckenmeyer.com

http://www.wedesignwise.com

notes from a developer

The most obvious limitation this style confronts is that of web-safe fonts. If this idea is new to you, I suggest you start by checking out typetester.org. This site will help you quickly understand just how limited typesetting is on the web. That being said, there are ways around it. Many of the tools for such purposes are presented in the Typography section of this book on page 129.

So, if your design relies heavily on typography, and especially if the content is being styled to be the showcase of the site, it is extremely pragmatic of you to design with basic web-safe fonts in mind. The most likely solution is a site that merges modern web type trickery and basic web-safe fonts.

http://www.nkbookreviews.com

http://www.min-style.de

http://www.unieq.nl

http://m1k3.net

http://www.gesteves.com

http://www.leandaryan.com

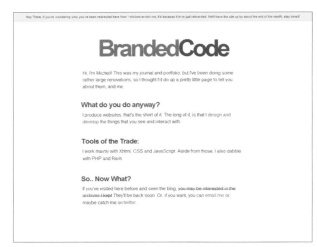

http://www.brandedcode.com

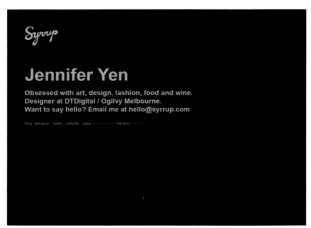

http://www.syrrup.com

http://de-online.co.uk

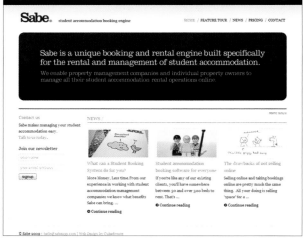

http://www.sabeapp.com

solid colors

Currently, there is a very popular pattern of using solid colors on web sites. That is to say, rather than using patterns or embellished containers, many designers are turning to a more basic approach and have been leveraging solid colors heavily. While there is not a lot to say about some deep meaning buried in the use of this style, we can make a few observations regarding how it is used.

The first is that though the style is "solid colors," this does not mean it must be used in an overly obsessive way; you can break your own self-prescribed rules. Remix (Figure 1) is the perfect example of this. While the design is largely based on the use of solid colors, you can see that it has but only a few actual solid colors in it. The trick in this case is subtle gradients that come darn close to being solid. The net result is a site design that is crisp, clean and downright beautiful.

Another prime example of the style being selectively applied is the IntuitionHQ site (Figure 2). Lots of dominant sections of solid color are offset by slick pseudo 3-D elements that help key parts of the design pop out. The designer gave the site additional depth with a gradient background and helped the logo pop by giving it a subtle shiny treatment. The trick to using a solid color style is finding the right balance between applying the style and breaking your own rules.

In other cases, the style is more literally applied. On the 99% site (Figure 3), for example, nearly all of the color applied to the site is solid and done via CSS background colors. This particular site is content heavy, and the design actually minimizes any distraction from the content. Additionally, with very few images to load, this solid color design makes for a really fast-loading page.

http://www.theglasgowcollective.com

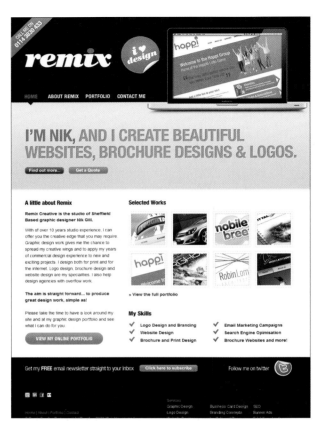

Figure 1 http://www.remixcreative.net

Figure 2 http://www.intuitionhq.com

http://www.alingham.com

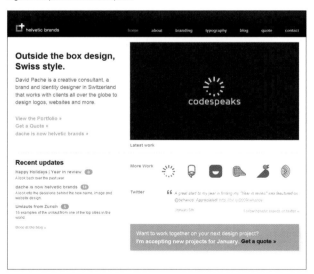

http://www.helveticbrands.ch

Figure 3 http://the99percent.com

http://www.kadlac.com

http://www.ibgdg.com

notes from a developer

It should come as no surprise to hear that sites using solid color designs are typically easy to implement, and this style is most likely going to produce sites that can load blindingly fast.

Let's contrast this with a much more visual style (like collage, wood or fabric styles). These styles rely on large and numerous images to piece together their layouts. With this, file sizes grow and loading a page takes much longer.

For those of us on high-speed connections, this might seem like a non-issue. But seconds count: There have been numerous studies to show that slower web sites equal lower revenue, for e-commerce sites, especially. This article from peer1.com spells out the problem: http://www.peer1.com/hosting/how-slow-websites-impact-visitors-and-sales.php.

So, a site designed in this style will play nicely when it comes to page load times, and it is a great design approach for extremely dynamic sites like e-commerce ones.

If you're wondering why your site is running slow, Yahoo!'s YSlow Firefox add-on is a fantastic tool: http://developer.yahoo.com/yslow.

I must also point out that more than the design, the quality of your web hosting will perhaps impact load time. Keep this in mind when you're tempted to go cheap on hosting.

http://rawkes.com

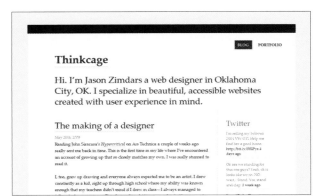

http://www.thinkcage.com

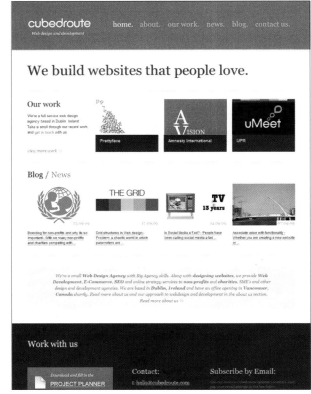

http://www.cubedroute.com

http://baltimoregreenworks.com

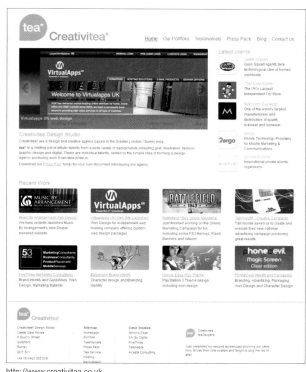

http://www.creativitea.co.uk

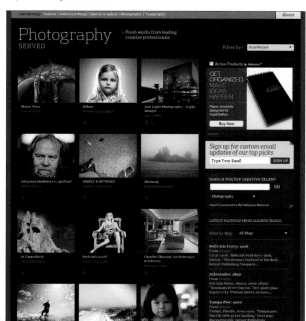

http://www.photographyserved.com

http://www.creativecomponent.com

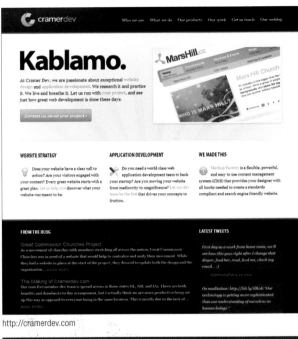

http://cramerdev.com

http://new.smilezonedentist.com

http://kolor-designs.com

fabric

A fabric-style site quite literally makes use of fabric as a part of the design. This distinct look seems to be nothing short of a popular trend, one that is finding its way into all types of sites. One of the key reasons I can see for this being the case is the same as with many other common styles: a need to break the digital mold and give the site an aesthetic that feels comfortable, inviting and just generally welcoming. Think of the industrial-style slab concrete benches found in many public spaces; while they might look nice in the big picture, they just aren't fun to sit on, and they certainly don't beckon you to relax and take it in. Sites that leverage an inviting style inevitably give a pleasant and welcoming aesthetic.

A prime example of this fabric-style design is the web site for Fourth Avenue Church (Figure 1). What more could a church hope for in its web site than to

be inviting, friendly and comfortable? It's such a logical connection that it isn't too difficult to see why a fabric style would make perfect sense. A common trend in church sites is a gritty, organic, splatter style, which communicates some similar elements that this homegrown fabric style does. Both say they are fresh, hip and keen to modern trends, but the latter does so with a bit more of a traditional style that doesn't alienate a fresh generation of churchgoers.

For a demonstration of a subtle way to leverage the style, take a look at the portfolio site for Tomaž Žlender (Figure 2). It is the dominant style of the site, and yet it is not overpowering. The textures of the fabrics bring this design to life and create a rich and elegant style. This type of approach is also found on the site of Bruno Duarte (Figure 3), where we find fabric in a supporting role of the design.

We again see how a fabric design style can offer a lively balance to a medium otherwise ruled by technology. What could be more low-tech than textiles?

http://feedstitch.com

Figure 1 http://fourthavenuechurch.org

Figure 2 http://www.tomazzlender.com

Figure 3 http://www.mormasso.com

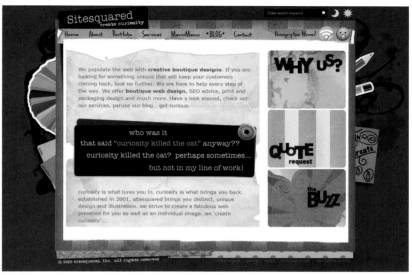

http://sitesquared.com

http://www.texturelovers.com

http://www.uniqueofficenyc.com

http://www.catherinecolebrook.com

notes from a developer

When it comes to implementation, fabric style sites raise one particular problem more than any other: image alignment. Many sites in this style rely on photographs or scanned bits of real fabric to create the composition. As such, it is likely that these designs will require pixel-perfect slicing and placement. This isn't totally unique to this style, but it is certainly a common factor. This isn't a showstopper, it just means your developer is going to spend a bit more time and energy getting it sliced up and properly aligned. I would also imagine this means you will have to pay careful attention to ensure it is properly translated into code.

If you want to help your developer, be mindful of elements at angles and ones that overlap others; if these items require transparency to interact, it will create some minor issues that also have to be surmounted. Remember, layers in a web page don't interact as rationally as they do in Photoshop. In fact, just to get transparency to work the way you expect it to requires a hack or two in order to make Internet Explorer cooperate.

http://www.ribbonsofred.com

http://www.uniqueofficenyc.com

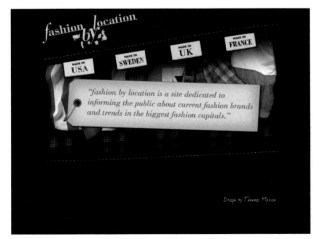

http://www.thomasmaxsondesign.com/project04/process/final

180

http://toriseye.quodis.com

http://broadersheet.com

http://www.gandrweb.com

http://www.eeci2009.com

http://www.lealea.net

http://www.kukkakontti.fi

http://www.ectomachine.com

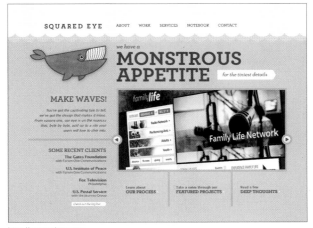

http://squaredeye.com

http://www.larissameek.com

http://www.scottboms.com

http://www.thespiritoftoys.com

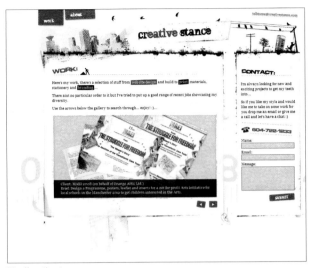

http://creativestance.com

wood

One of the most compelling reasons to use wood textures in a site design is for the purpose of creating a certain atmosphere. Wood can no doubt be used in a purely aesthetic way, to simply dress up the page. So what kind of atmospheres can wood establish? The range is quite dramatic, so let's look at a few examples.

The Kinetic Technology Group web site (Figure 1) has made prominent usage of wood as a visual element, and the result is remarkably effective. I actually come from an IT background, having worked as a network engineer for some time, and as such am pretty familiar with the stigma the industry carries. Let's face it, no one calls for IT support unless something is broken. Because of that, a bit of a negative and impersonal aura has formed around the industry. The use of wood in this case helps humanize the company. Instead of a band of uber-nerds that will mock you for your foolishness, you get what appears to be a company employing normal people who just want to help. And take careful note of the style of wood used—it isn't a pretentious designer wood, but rather a down-home, everyday, normal kind of wood.

The Rocky Creek Winery site (Figure 2) leverages wood for a very different atmosphere. Here, the design is classy, but just shy of luxurious. The winery comes off as a nice establishment, without appearing overly snooty. And there are the obvious connections to nature and barrels in which wine is aged, enhancing the effectiveness of the design style.

The personal site of Brent Lafreniere (Figure 3) uses wood mostly for decorative purposes, but it does lend itself to a casual atmosphere—one that is echoed in other small ways, like the playful illustration at the top and the lack of capital letters in the large welcome statement. These elements all combine to produce an approachable design that no doubt reflects the personality of the individual behind the site.

Figure 2 http://www.rockycreekwinery.ca

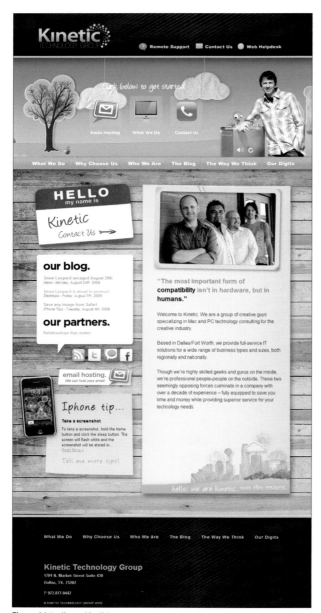

Figure 1 http://www.kinetictg.com

Figure 3 http://www.tnerb.com

http://www.focadesign.com.br

http://mariuszciesla.com

notes from a developer

When it comes to the use of wood images in your design, one of the things your developer most likely will need from you is a repeating background. This is one of those cases where you can let the developer sort it out and hope it looks like what you want, or you can plan ahead and make sure those wood backgrounds repeat properly, making life easy for your developer and ensuring the results you want.

One solution is to make the wood image huge, but this just causes other issues. The preferred method is to use a somewhat smaller image and repeat it. Many designers I talk to have no idea how to create a repeating image. It seems like an impossible task until you figure out the offset filter in Photoshop. This article from Tutorial Blog describes the process perfectly: http://tutorialblog.org/make-repeating-seamless-tile-backgrounds-with-photoshop.

Tackling this ahead of time is a great way not only to support your developer, but to make her love you for being prepared.

http://www.truckhunt.com

http://www.ernesthemingwaycollection.com

http://www.bcandullo.com

http://www.jonnyhaynes.com

http://www.chanellehenry.com

http://cellarthief.com

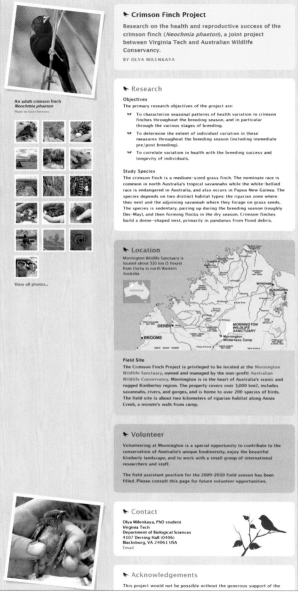

http://www.milenkaya.org

http://www.arunpattnaik.com

http://www.professionalkitchensnj.com

http://www.mikeprecious.com/work/index.php?workdetail=wb-candybouquet

http://parkplacetexas.com

http://www.ltmoses.com

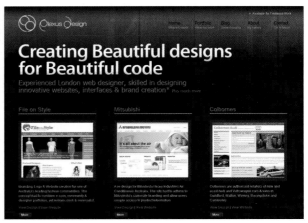

http://www.plexusdesign.co.uk

06/

atypical navigation • atypical layouts •
pseudo-flash • horizontal scrolling • one-page

sites by structural styles

If I could suggest a single section of this book to someone to encourage them into new ways of thinking, it would be this section. It seems there are often two sides to a debate over structure. One dictates that doing anything that might be dubbed "atypical" is wrong and creates poor usability. The other side is driven to break the rules and find solutions that work, but don't stay within the lines. This is what I love about this section: the topics force us to reconsider things. Does the main navigation have to be at the top? Does a site require more than one page? What if I scrolled the page horizontally? So many hot topics, so little time. These are the sections that have always created the most tension on Design Meltdown and have always had the most interest; I think it is because they provide some serious inspiration value.

atypical navigation

The notion of breaking the norm, setting new patterns and generally creating a truly fresh web site inevitably leads designers to experimenting with alternate forms of navigation. As with many such experiments, this often leads to bizarre and unusable solutions. But out of such exploration can come new methods that actually make a site not only more interesting, but often more usable.

The use of the word "atypical" in titling this section suggests that there are some norms that these sites go against—this is true. Typical sites have the logo in the top left, main links across the top, login links in the top right, and secondary navigation down the left. All these are norms that many users and designers have come to embrace. So why break the norm in the first place? Usability is the only legitimate reason.

Ironically, if a design has good or bad usability, it might not be as obvious at times on sites that use this style. Such is the case with the JPEG Interactive site (Figure 2). Here, we find a very unusual navigation system that can only be fully understood as you use it. In this case, the process of getting to the information is half the art of the site. Considering the type of work the agency does, this is a perfect embodiment of the type of work they would like to attract. Another great example of this going-against-the-norm style is the Nalin Design site (Figure 1), where again we find a very unique system of navigation.

For what might be considered a more practical demonstration of this style, take a look at the personal site of Benny Martinson (Figure 3). Here, the primary navigation has been boiled down to three main links. Instead of the typical landing page full of content, the user is quickly and easily guided to the main section she is in search of—more information, his portfolio or his contact information.

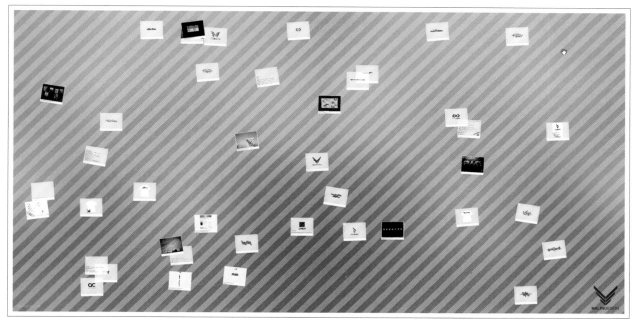

Figure 1 http://www.nalindesign.com

Figure 1 (close up) http://www.nalindesign.com

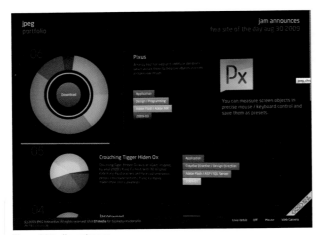

Figure 2 http://www.jpeg.cn

Figure 3 http://www.bennymartinson.com

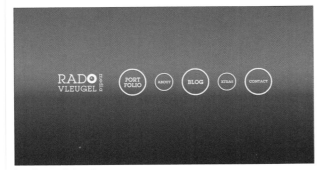

http://www.radovleugel.com

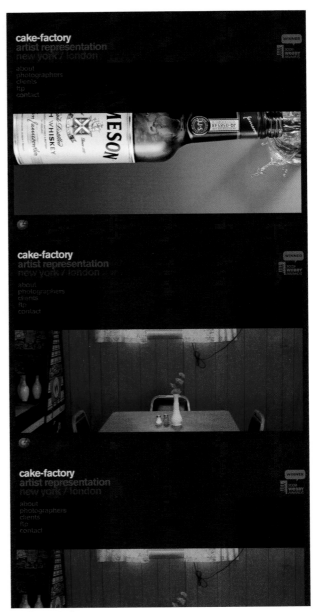

http://www.cake-factory.com

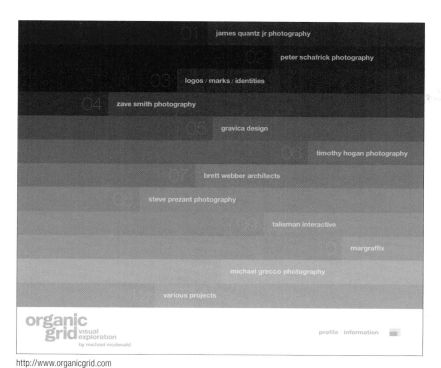

http://www.organicgrid.com

http://www.1.nalindesign.com

http://searchinsidevideo.com

http://andyshaw.me

http://www.sarahmoody.org.uk

http://www.rsabroker.com/movingstories

http://www.uberdm.com

notes from a developer

There is perhaps nothing more exciting—and, at the same time, nothing more annoying—than a designer reinventing navigation. The pragmatic developer will scoff at breaking the norms. The visionary developer will see the challenge and rise to the occasion.

As you design your site using atypical navigation, never lose sight of the user's experience. If your crazy interface approach makes the site impossible to use, you better reconsider. As you take this approach, it is important to have an open mind and to be prepared for some really negative feedback. This is most certainly not a style that should be chosen flippantly. The best uses of it do so for a reason, and the navigation adds to the experience and doesn't detract from it.

If you want to let people explore your product in a new way so they can understand how it works, atypical navigation just might be the answer. On the other hand, if you're building an e-commerce site, you better be extremely careful before you try something wacky, as you might prevent anyone from making it through your "cool" checkout system.

atypical layouts

It seems that the very notion of a layout being branded atypical sparks all sorts of responses. Many people are annoyed by it and find it to be total rubbish, while others see it as refreshing and the challenging way of thinking they were looking for. So, I present to you a set of some of the finest examples of atypical layouts I have found.

The BigKid site (Figure 1) has a simple and completely nonstandard layout. There isn't really anything about the layout that resembles the norm except that you can find the logo in the top left. Somehow, the design has managed to transform its content into what feels like a work of art. Perhaps it is the beautiful photographs, or the frame-like containers. Whatever the case, this design serves as a great portal to the content, fills the screen to make as much of it visible as possible, and just generally serves its purpose beautifully. I love that its alternative layout style doesn't detract from its usability.

The Paddocks Education site (Figure 2) demonstrates this style in a practical way. On some key elements, the site sticks to tried-and-true layout mechanics: the logo is in the top left, primary navigation is across the top, the key call to action is near the top left, and key info and links are in the footer. Yet the content region of this site mixes things up enough so as not to look like every other site. Here, the designer was liberal enough to push the limits, and at the same time leverage some common patterns.

http://www.nextbigleap.com

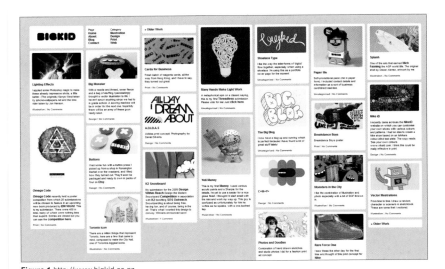

Figure 1 http://www.bigkid.co.nz

http://www.grondecki.pl

http://www.multiways.com

Figure 2 http://paddockseducation.com

hello,
my name is fran rosa and
this is the largest collection ever
of my work as a designer and some
personal and student projects

ref. 058 **44th heinoken jazzaldia** poster design for this jazz festival contest submission	ref. 056 **cases museu, del privat al públic** brochure for this seminar organized by caixa catalunya and universitat de barcelona for rsb media	ref. 053 **rsb media** concept logos for the new identity of this interactive agency for rsb media
ref. 053 **rsb media** concept logos for the new identity of this interactive agency for rsb media	ref. 052 **turismo y cooperación al desarrollo en el mediterráneo** design of this book published by libertar for rsb media	ref. 051 **20 anys dels cursos de gestió cultural a la universitat de barcelona** logo for this anniversary for rsb media	ref. 049 **yves rocher** campaign for this brand of natural beauty for rsb media
ref. 048 **otra navidad es posible** xmas self-promotion campaign for interactive agency rsb media for rsb media	ref. 047 **nos movemos** new office informative mailing for interactive agency rsb media for rsb media	ref. 046 **using** corporate website restyling for this usability services company for rsb media	ref. 045 **shareing** website and identity for this trip sharing community for rsb media
7 días por 99 céntimos mailing campaign for dating service friendscout24 for rsb media	ref. 043 **fátima carmena** website for this cinematographer, photographer, producer and journalist personal project	ref. 042 **associació catalana de tècnics en prevenció de riscos laborals** logo for this profesional association freelance	ref. 041 **maemo.org** logo for this community contest submission
ref. 040 **mediterranean consulting** corporate website for this consultancy firm freelance	ref. 039 **conciertos en la iglesia de san nicolás** poster announcing seasonal concerts organized by sanmadmadrid freelance	ref. 038 **soma compilation 2008** cover design for soma records techno music compilation contest submission	ref. 037 **ya (nos) veremos** fictional short film about a casual encounter in barcelona city student project
ref. 036 **loop barcelona** website and identity for this videoart festival student project	ref. 035 **dolce vita barcelona** website for this free fashion shopping guide student project	ref. 034 **data portability project** logo for this initiative contest submission	ref. 033 **servicios de consultoría para el sector textil** services for textile industry brochure for mediterranean consulting freelance
ref. 032 **blogstorming** istitute europeo di design barcelona students community blog design student project	ref. 031 **mediterranean consulting** slideshows for this consultancy firm freelance	ref. 030 **basi** design of this documentation and production management tool for dressmaking workshops decentralized network basi freelance	ref. 029 **stories form the field** logo for the united nations documentary film festival contest submission
ref. 028 **movement of jam people** book about bob marley and the wailers exodus album student project	ref. 027 **a pelo** logo for this ecological textile company student project	ref. 026 **vivera** website and identity for this online community for artists student project	ref. 025 **ciutat vella** identity for the barcelona district called ciutat vella and its four neighbourhoods student project
ref. 024 **ideas** logo for this hosting company personal project	ref. 023 **sevasa** corporate website for this engraved crystal glass producer for dilema	ref. 022 **irla.cat** website for josep irla foundation for caixa alta	ref. 021 **polinyà medi ambient** signal design for polinyà selective collection containers for dilema
ref. 020 **colegio profesional de ingenieros en informática de castilla y león** logo for this ict professional corporation contest submission	ref. 019 **les crisis oblidades** website for this carnet jove (euro<20) solidarity project for dilema	ref. 018 **i jornades sobre el consum sostenible i responsable a catalunya** collateral for this seminar organized by agència catalana de consum for dilema	ref. 017 **llibreria serret** online shop and forum for this bookshop for dilema
ref. 016 **cemsa** packaging for this depilatory wax manufacturer for dilema	ref. 015 **cemsa** product catalogues for this depilatory wax manufacturer for dilema	ref. 014 **alumestil** logo for this aluminium related company projecte personal	ref. 013 **cemsa** corporate website for this depilatory wax manufacturer for dilema
ref. 012 **botiga jerc** t-shirts for jerc online shop on topics like independentism	ref. 011 **anubis cosmetics** corporate website for this cosmetics manufacturer for dilema	ref. 010 **ajuntament d'esparreguera** website for esparreguera city council for dilema	ref. 009 **iguapop** website for this concert promoter company for digit

http://visualkultura.com

http://realtimeracing.org

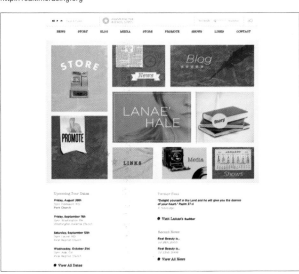

http://www.lanaehale.com/home

notes from a developer

In contrast to the section on Atypical Navigation on page 194, this style will not likely get nearly as negative a response from your developer. On the surface, many developers will object to doing something outside the norm, but if your design is practical and focuses on the user's needs, it will likely be well received. In many ways, developers are far more creative than they get credit for—it's just that their creativity comes in solving technical problems and not visual ones. All the same, a good programmer can understand the notion of good design. And if your design embraces the user's needs and improves functionality by breaking the norms of page layout, you probably have something worth pursuing. Your best bet is to present your atypical layout design in the context of how functional it is, not how original it is.

http://www.digitalic.org/portfolio

http://www.tmsportmanagement.com

http://www.rdbrown.me.uk

http://www.xische.com

http://f91w.com

http://www.finalcutters.com

http://www.lyricalmedia.com

http://www.nvlstudio.com

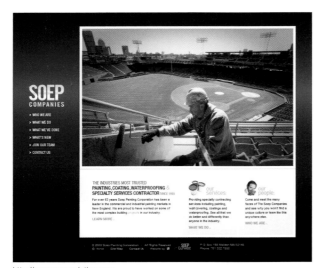

http://www.soeppainting.com

http://www.rabbleandrouser.com

http://www.classicsapp.com

http://designspasm.net

pseudo-flash

It isn't that Flash is going away or somehow falling out of popularity, but there is a sharp increase in the number of sites displaying Flash-like functionality via good, old-fashioned JavaScript. The refinement of tools such as jQuery, script.aculo.us and MochiKit has provided ways to quickly build such functionality, saving both time and money.

In many cases, this Flash-like style shows up in small ways, like navigation elements that fade in and out as you hover over them, or slick bubble pop-ups as you mouse over something. Countless small things have been done to provide more interactive aspects of a site that create beautiful flourishes and bring a design to life. This section will focus on a slightly more ambitious use of the style. The samples collected here manage to emulate an entirely Flash-based site and offer interfaces that make the user presume he is looking at a Flash site.

So why go to all this trouble to make an HTML and CSS site behave like a Flash one? I can think of two obvious reasons. The first is skill sets. Flash is a niche in the web industry that can drive entire careers. It takes a lot of time to learn to do it right, and even more time to actually build stuff. Given the combination of technical and visual skills required, it is perhaps one of the most difficult aspects of web development. As such, many more people have become familiar with JavaScript and, as a result, this is simply a more viable option.

The second, and perhaps most likely, reason for the increase in Flash-like designs is SEO—good old search engine optimization. Yes, many great developments have been made to enable Flash-based content to be indexed by search engines, and, yes, there are a number of ways to make it work. But the question I always come back to is if SEO is the goal, why bother with a platform that makes you work so hard? And that's the real beauty of these sites; under the hood, they are straightforward HTML, styled up with CSS and animated with JavaScript. This means search engines see all the content in its unstyled format with no additional effort.

The pragmatic developer in me can't resist loving this solution. This approach is becoming more and more popular and is likely to be very common in coming years.

http://www.siebennull.com

http://www.floridaflourish.com

http://www.tuckinteractiv.com

http://eyedraw.eu

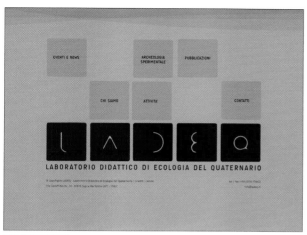

http://www.ladeq.it

http://www.howarths.nl

notes from a developer

As a designer, this approach is very tempting, but I would suggest a healthy dose of caution as you consider embarking on such a site. Not only is it quite likely to be much more expensive and time consuming than you might expect, but it will probably also be quite difficult to implement.

This is another situation where the more experience you have in actually building web sites, the better equipped you are to make use of this style. A great way to take baby steps into this style is to familiarize yourself with the types of effects jQuery can perform. By studying the types of effects available, you can be sure to design around known factors as opposed to pie-in-the-sky ideas. Dig through the jQuery effects library here: http://api.jquery.com/category/effects.

There is nothing quite as powerful as going to your developer with your design in hand and corresponding examples of code that does what you're looking for. Not only does it spell it out for your developer and communicate exactly what you're looking for, it also shows a level of respect for the developer's world and demonstrates that you want to play nice with what is realistic.

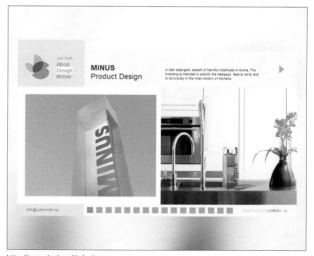

http://www.joshsmithdesign.com

207

http://www.seankeenan.org.uk

http://www.gavincastleton.com

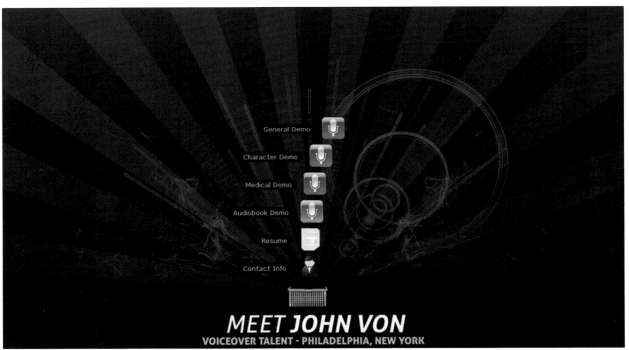

http://meetjohnvon.com

http://www.johnantoni.com

http://www.alexarts.ru/en

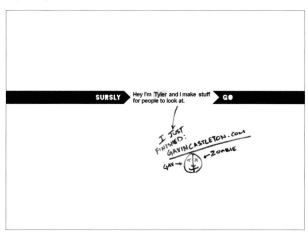

http://www.sursly.com

http://www.chameleon-home.com

horizontal scrolling

For many designers the notion of a horizontal scrolling site is not even a possibility—it's an approach that never enters their minds. This is perhaps for good reason, as it breaks a firmly ingrained user expectation of scrolling up and down; however, there are many cases where it can be used with great success. Claire Baxter's personal site is one such example (Figure 1).

On Claire's site, we see how a single-page site can be transformed into a quick-responding site that is like a traditional site with many pages, but with the benefit of a nice page-to-page transition. This is one of those sites you simply have to use to really love. It responds super fast, flows really well and is crystal clear. Amazingly, this site avoids even the least bit of confusion that might result from scrolling side to side.

Sites that showcase photography, such as Melissa Marie Hernandez's portfolio, can be very well-served by a horizontal scrolling site (Figure 2). Photographs work particularly well in this style, as they line up so perfectly and make for a beautiful strip of images. On Melissa's site, the size and flow of the photographs means that the next image peeks out at you, enticing you to keep clicking. This hint of what is to come drove me to shuffle through the galleries, and this is certainly what the owner wants potential clients to do.

One place that it would seem rather unlikely to find a horizontal scrolling site would be in the real-estate industry, but this is just the case with the Pinchot Forest web site (Figure 3). In addition to being another example of a page with a smooth-moving side scroll, it also has the interesting feature of a static menu bar. Many sites like this repeat the navigation on each frame as it moves, and others force you to return to the homepage to dig into other content. Instead, this site simply slides the content along with the logo and navigation anchored in place. This is a wonderful use of the style that doesn't detract from usability and makes for a unique experience.

Figure 1 http://www.vanityclaire.com

Figure 2 http://www.melissamariehernandez.com

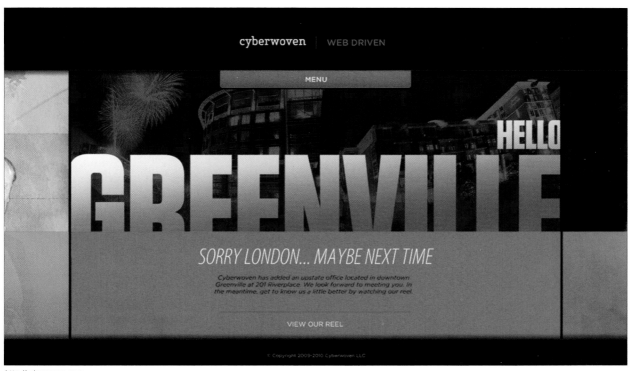

http://cyberwoven.com

Figure 3 http://www.pinchotforest.com

As a developer, I have had a wide range of designs brought to me ready to be coded. But this is one style I have yet to implement in code myself. I can tell you that the day a designer tells me this is his grand idea, he will probably see me roll my eyes and let out a small sigh. This approach can create huge usability issues, as well as technical snafus.

In particular, suppressing the vertical scroll bar and just showing a horizontal one might sound simple, but it isn't so cut and dried. Considering that most browsers are designed to allow users to scroll vertically to see content, you have to be careful when you start overriding this behavior.

If this is truly the direction you want to go, carefully consider the size of your content and how it will show up on browsers when they aren't full-screen on your fancy 30-inch monitor. If you can design within reasonable limitations in this regard, your developer is likely to be a lot more open to the approach.

http://www.hasrimy.com

http://www.avilasoto.com

http://album.alexflueras.ro

one-page

The one-page site has so many obvious purposes, it is difficult to figure out what can be said or done with it that's actually new or fresh. Remarkably, though, the examples provided here actually manage to feel totally fresh and unique.

Many of the samples rely on overall minimal styles, which very effectively complement the minimalist notion of a single-page web site. Many of the sites featured here could easily have had several pages, and the designers would have been driven to fluff up the content to fill the space. Instead, a focus on efficiency and ease of use dominates the end result, which features content that is easy to consume, quick to load and keen on satisfying the user with all the information she needs.

A perfect example of this is the portfolio site of Jack Bloom (Figure 1). This one-page site does many things remarkably well. For starters, it is certainly in a semi-minimalistic style. I say semi because it does have some flourish and embellishment, but overall it is bare bones. For example, the text itself is rendered in creative and beautiful ways, allowing it to serve two roles: decoration and content.

There is another potential strategy in putting all of the content in a single page. The NineFlavors (Figure 2) site is a single-page site that uses a sort of in-line scrolling to change out the content. On first glance, this is kind of clever and feels nice. But it does lead to the inevitable question: Why not just put each content bit on its own page? There are

many possible answers, and I want to focus on one that seems like a different perspective. As a design agency, it can be quite difficult to get people to thumb through all of your content, samples and history in order to sell them on you as an agency. In this case, if the user takes the first step and clicks a link, he is surprised that the content just pops in. Somehow it feels like less of a time investment than going through multiple pages. As a user, I am quickly enticed to click all the links and thereby run through all the content. So this is a great way to make it simple for someone to get a quick overview of a fair amount of content. It reduces the sensation of surfing around a big mass and needing to get orientated.

Figure 1 http://oldergraphicdesigner.com

Figure 2 http://www.nineflavors.com

http://www.kaabstudios.com

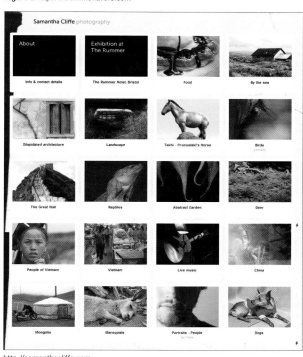

http://samanthacliffe.com

http://socialsnack.com

http://www.holtedesign.no

http://www.contrabrand.net

http://www.brian-eagan.com

http://lancamjewellery.co.uk

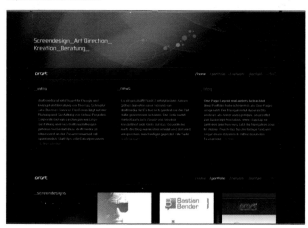

http://www.draftmedia.de

http://pixelmanya.com

http://www.thismortalmagic.com

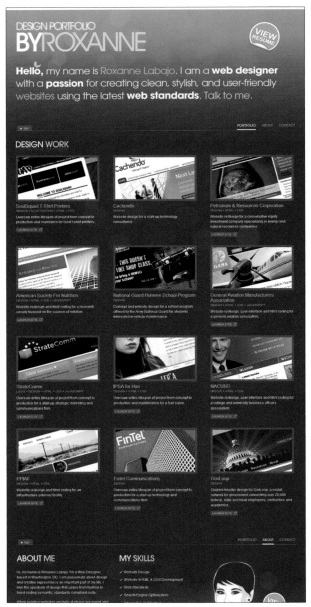

http://byroxanne.com

http://www.ultimate-media.nl

http://www.brizk.com

http://www.fajnechlopaki.com

http://www.gnoso.com

07/

sites by
structural elements

One great way to break down design is by function. This approach can be so handy for finishing a design; seldom will you start the inspiration process here. But ultimately you will include some widget in your design and start out on a mission to find fresh ideas. In a way, this section of the book represents trends from a slightly different perspective. For example, the level of quality found in the jQuery UI controls means we find many more accordions in use (not that there was a shortage, but they really have had a boom). Even something as common as tabs have found even more use simply because they are technically easier to accomplish. The modern web has us piecing together many components created by others, making the process of customization and leveraging fresh ideas all the more important.

tabs

Tabs are a basic way to organize web content, and they provide a visual cue as to how that content is grouped. They are also quite often a means of indicating where you are in a site. As such, these heavily used items have been styled every way you might imagine, and yet we can still find some fresh examples to inspire us to venture into new territory.

Tabs can unifiy a design via repetition, as seen on the ClothMoth site (Figure 1). Here, the buttons echo the fabric theme and kitschy style of the site. The tabs are used to echo the standard tag found in clothing, and they thereby become a functional part of the theme and usage of the site. While this design overall might not push the envelope, it certainly is well thought out and effectively put to work.

Another thing that is always great to see is a theme that is extended to every aspect of a design. More often than not, tabs are put to work without deep meanings and dual purposes. Such is the case with Fran Boot's site (Figure 2) and The CSS Blog (Figure 3) site. These sites don't do anything revolutionary with their tabs, but all the same they work as a seamless part of the design.

Some designers make tabs do interesting things, like a side menu that looks like an oblong tab, as seen on the IM Design (Figure 4) and MetaLab (Figure 5) sites. These designs make a side menu appear as tabs as well as simple links. This converts a standard side menu into one that helps you understand your location within the site, which is something very helpful for people landing on sub pages via a search engine or shared link.

http://quirkylotus.com

Figure 1 http://www.clothmoth.com

Figure 2 http://www.narfstuff.co.uk/portfolio

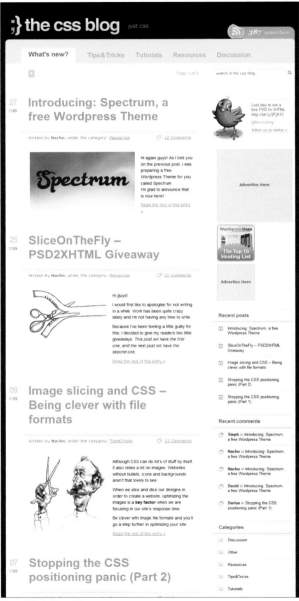

Figure 3 http://thecssblog.com

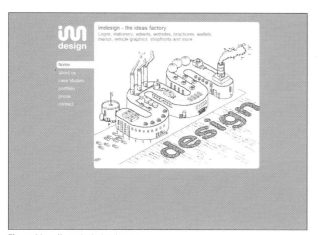

Figure 4 http://www.imdesignuk.com

Figure 5 http://www.metalabdesign.com

http://www.msites.com

http://www.piensaenpixels.com

http://www.manisheriar.com

One of the most common ways to create tabs is known as the sliding window technique, which involves styling regular lists into beautiful tabs with background images that slide into place. A very thorough write-up of this technique can be found on A List Apart: www.alistapart.com/articles/slidingdoors.

This approach will either combine real live text with background images, or it will embed the text into the images themselves. Neither of these approaches is too difficult, and they both can be built to be fairly flexible. However, given that tabs are typically horizontal, they suffer from space limitations and should therefore be planned out carefully.

Tabs are a problem that have been solved in many ways with jQuery (http://jqueryui.com/demos/tabs). The main reason to go this route is if you need the tabs to act as part of the content and change what the user sees without a page load; CSS tabs are a part of the page template that really just lead to whole new pages.

buttons

If you're reading this section, you're likely designing some buttons for a site and wondering what has been done to this simple control. You're also probably wondering how to retain functionality but dress it up so it doesn't look like a boring default button. After all, we can't just let it have its default style—that's no fun.

Some sites apply pretty standard styles and dress up buttons to a point that improves visibility and eases site use, as seen on the sites for Airbnb (Figure 1) and Notable (Figure 3). These buttons are pretty standard in terms of style, but they fit the designs well, improve visibility and certainly avoid a misplaced default style.

Other sites do interesting things, such as visually combining two buttons into one, like on Go Freelance's site (Figure 2). Others, like MailChimp (Figure 4)

and NCover (Figure 5), pack a lot of extra info in and make them into uber buttons. These supersized buttons contain a lot of content and are physically large in size. In this way, they not only communicate something, but also have space to tell you precisely what you will get by clicking through. This can be a very effective way to draw attention and drive people to a desired action on the web site.

It is no surprise to see that in all of these examples the buttons have become larger and far more visible than the default style a button might have. And they still demonstrate that an often-ignored element can be leveraged in powerful ways to achieve desired results.

Also, take a look at the Forms chapter of this book on page 229, as many of the forms shown there have a wide range of custom-designed buttons.

http://www.ascendsport.com

http://www.nanastreak.com/webdesignersidea/eBandLive

Figure 1 http://www.airbnb.com

Figure 2 http://www.gofreelance.org

Figure 3 http://www.notableapp.com

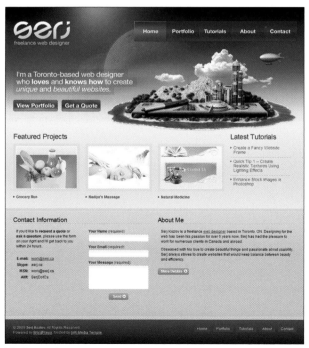

http://www.serj.ca

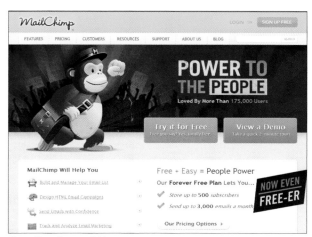

Figure 4 http://www.mailchimp.com

Figure 5 http://www.ncover.com

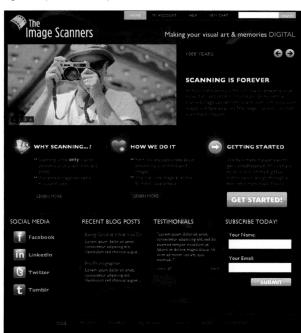

http://theimagescanners.com

http://www.sonarhq.com

http://www.uploadpie.com

http://www.storenvy.com

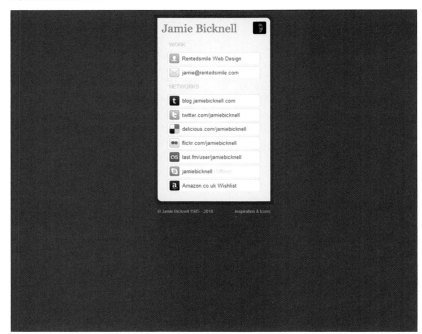

http://www.jamiebicknell.com

http://www.1stchoiceaccommodations.com

http://www.classicplanestv.com

form elements

There is no other basic HTML element as problematic as form controls. Form controls include text boxes, drop-down lists, radio buttons, check boxes and buttons. These have long been the bane of developers, because designers inevitability want to do seemingly simple things to dress them up. Much like with typography on the web, though, the more you understand the constraints these elements come with, the better you can design around them. The samples provided here prove that forms can be beautiful and extremely functional.

On the site for GuiFied (Figure 1), we find standard form controls fixed up and looking beautiful. The first thing to note about these controls is their size. Since the number of fields is relatively short, making the controls large is not much of a problem. These large controls ensure that it is easy to use; there is nothing more annoying than trying to read what you have typed into a tiny text box. There is nothing too radical in this site's form designs, but they have been meshed into the design of the site very effectively.

The Kartel site (Figure 2) demonstrates another interesting approach to beautifying form controls. Instead of tweaking the form elements, the designers have simply manipulated the surrounding elements where they have far more control. These controls look almost like the default styles render them, and yet they mesh perfectly with their streamlined containers. This is a perfect demonstration of working within the limitations in an effort to save time and money.

Other sites go to great lengths to make form controls behave in unbelievable ways. Take the Firsthost sign-up form (Figure 3), for instance. The slider controls used on this page are effectively radio buttons, as they only allow the user to select a single option. The result is ultimately the same, so why bother with such complexities (besides the fact that the developer most likely geeked out over this in a major way)? In this case, I would suggest that the slider makes it more obvious that you're changing something substantial. The slider reminds the user that she is not only selecting something new, but essentially leaving something else behind. This slider approach helps the user see and understand how her changes impact the final cost.

Figure 1 http://guified.com

Figure 2 http://www.kartel.co.nz

http://www.traditionalboundaries.com

http://www.iseatz.com

Figure 3 http://www.firehost.com

http://strutta.com

notes from a developer

Forms are perhaps one of the most painful HTML elements to deal with. Not only do they render very differently in every browser, but they also accept and apply CSS in very inconsistent ways. It is most likely that you will hear some grumbling from your developer if you design fancy forms with rounded corners, drop shadows and inner glows.

This is a great place to pick your battles. Are extremely custom forms necessary? Perhaps subtle upgrades are more than sufficient. Of course, you might be trying to make an important form in a header or footer mesh with the site. If this is the case, there are a few work-arounds to accommodate most any design. I will also say that this is one of those cases where almost anything really is possible; it's all a matter of cost. Don't believe me? Check out the ComponentArt controls: www.componentart.com/products/silverlight/editors.

Niceforms (www.emblematiq.com/lab/niceforms) is a handy script that lets you give forms a total visual overhaul. jQuery is your friend in this area for sure; for example, check out jqTransform (www.dfc-e.com/metiers/multimedia/opensource/jqtransform) to help your text areas grow (www.unwrongest.com/projects/elastic). And we cannot cover this topic and leave out the jQuery UI library (http://jqueryui.com/demos) or the Yahoo! UI Library (http://developer.yahoo.com/yui).

http://wpcoder.com

http://graphik.fi

http://www.ecolect.net

http://www.behance.net

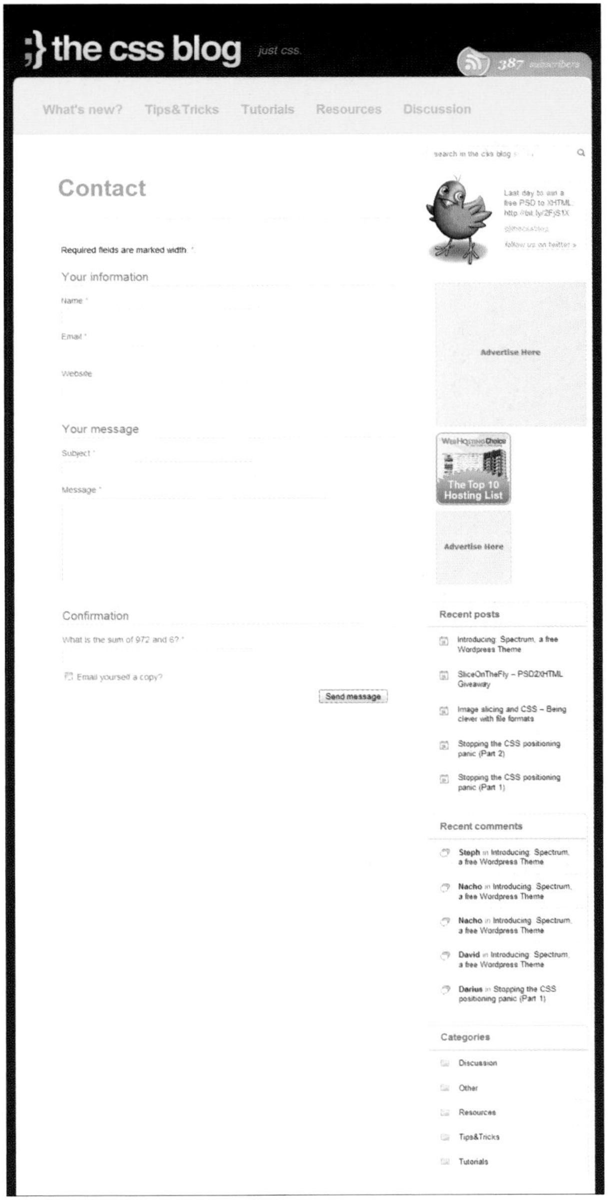

http://thecssblog.com

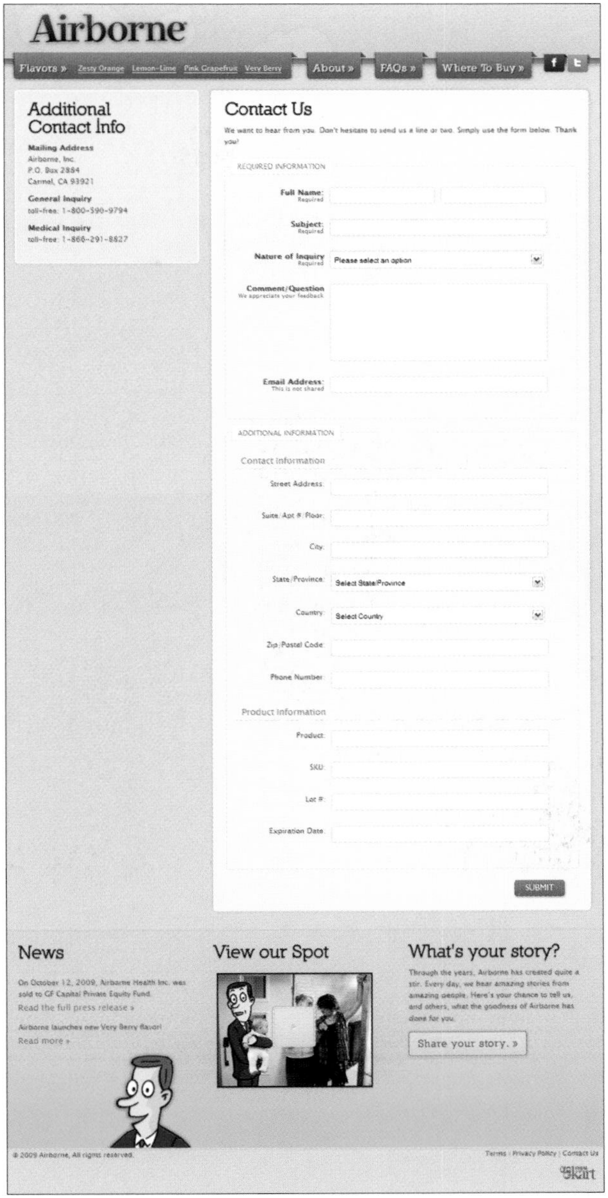

http://www.airbornehealth.com

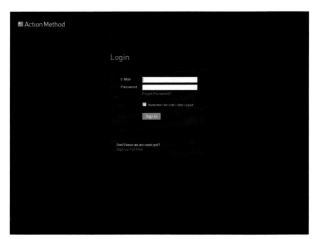

http://www.actionmethod.com

http://www.campaignhq.co.nz

http://www.holdsworthdesign.com

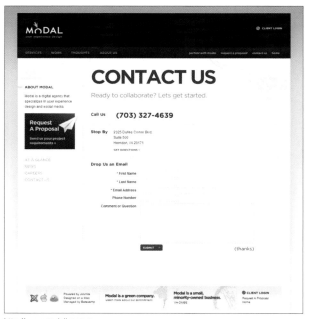

http://www.modalinc.com

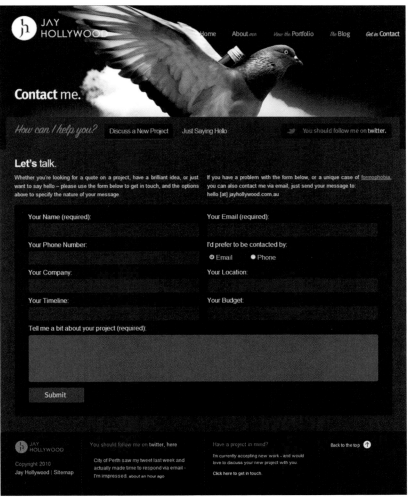

http://www.jayhollywood.com.au

helpful homepages

This section cannot exist without mentioning user experience, which takes us into a topic that can easily fill a book. For this small commentary on the topic, I want to consider some homepages that don't necessarily fit the norms and why I think they are demonstrations of truly helpful homepages.

Let's start with the Bohemian Coding site (Figure 1). Not only is the design clean with incredibly clear imagery, it's also very helpful. Instead of bloating the page with sales pitches on all their products, or why their development process is so great, they simply guide you to the content you're searching for. In this way, the user easily digs a bit deeper to learn about the software that interests him most. A design such as this focuses on the user's needs, not the shop's need to show what they wished visitors thought was important. Several of the other examples in this chapter also use this minimalistic guiding technique.

The LA Music Blog site (Figure 2) not only has a helpful homepage, it also sets a better standard for a niche that typically sucks. Content portals such as calendars and city blogs tend to get bloated and unusable. Here, a lot of content is presented, but it is so clearly broken down that it is still easy to skim and consume. The color coding helps the user zone in on the content and almost becomes a muscle memory sort of response.

A slightly different strategy can be found on the Blend site (Figure 3). This homepage pulls a few key bits of information from each section to the homepage, almost like a teaser to pull you into each bucket as appropriate. Here, the clarity of hierarchy really helps keep it usable.

There are endless possibilities for homepages, and the small set here shows the extreme range of successful options. As always, the key is to focus on the consumers and what they want most out of your site. One of the most helpful things can be to look at log files and figure out which pages are the most popular; then just make it easier on the users and create a homepage that helps them find that content faster.

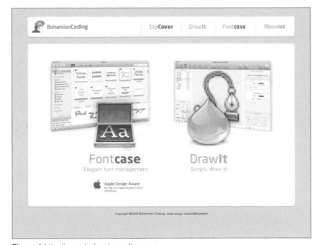

Figure 1 http://www.bohemiancoding.com

Figure 2 http://lamusicblog.com

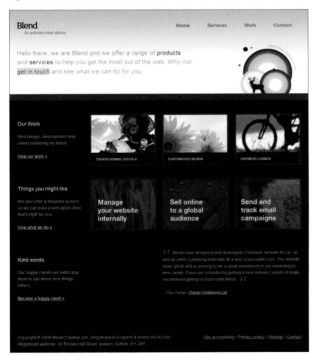

Figure 3 http://www.blend.uk.com

http://www.elixirgraphics.com

http://www.seydesign.com

http://www.needanelectrician.co.nz

http://www.nanastreak.com/webdesignersidea/LowertownPrintingCompany

http://www.lindtexcellence.com

http://www.taoeffect.com

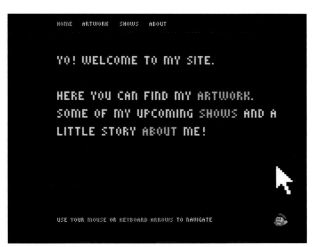

http://www.teoskaffa.com

functional footers

Footers can be one of the most neglected portions of a web site. Quite often, their content is limited to some copyright text, perhaps a few key links, maybe a logo and the typical links to legal pages. The irony of these bare-bones footers is that after a user gets to the bottom of a page (which is a sign that he consumed the contents instead of clicking away), he is left with no direction of what else to do. Many designers have figured this out and have started making very functional footers that kindly direct people to additional content.

It seems that a natural by-product of making a functional footer is that it grows in size. Some can take up an entire screen all themselves, begging the question: Where does the footer start and end? For example, on Jason Santa Maria's site (Figure 1), he almost has two footers: the typical boring one and a content-filled helpful one. These key items help guide the reader to other useful sections of the site, almost like a mini homepage portal.

The footer on the Fusionware Design site (Figure 2) contains a somewhat unique element: a contact form. Typically, contact forms land on their own page, but instead the site really encourages the reader to contact them by placing the contact form at the bottom of every single page. Another thing in this footer that is rather atypical is a call to action. Most functional footers have pointers to other relevant content, newsletter sign-up forms and other peripheral content; but here, it has a key call to action and, even better, the actual means to do it. This is a direction I have seldom seen in site design, but it makes perfect sense.

http://rockbeatspaper.com

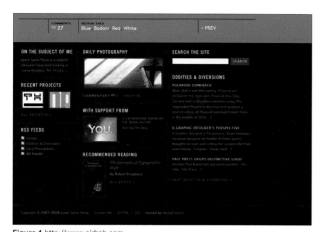

Figure 1 http://www.airbnb.com

http://www.jointmedias.com

Figure 2 http://fusionwaredesign.com

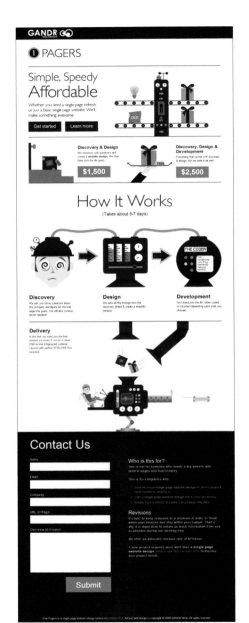

http://gandrweb.com/one

http://kolor-designs.com/blog

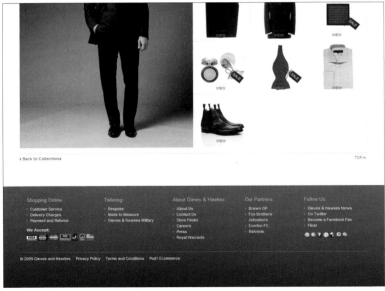

http://www.gievesandhawkes.com

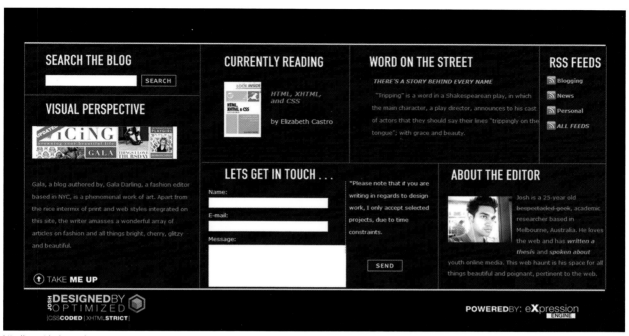

http://www.trippingwords.com

http://www.endoscopia.com

http://elliotjaystocks.com

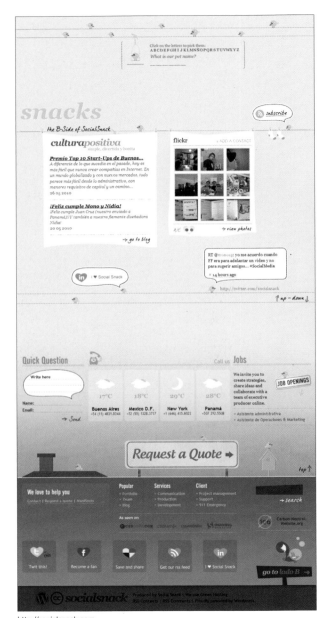

http://socialsnack.com

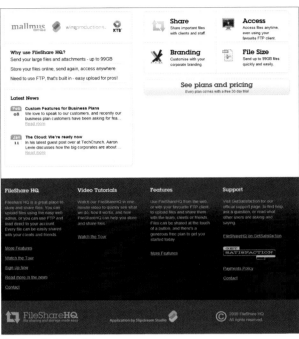

http://www.filesharehq.com

http://designmess.com

http://www.raddsigns.com

http://bradcolbow.com

homepage slide shows

The homepage slide show has become an incredibly common component of many web sites. I can see two main reasons for this. One, it isn't too difficult to create. There are many scripts out there that make this a very simple process. The other reason for the prevalence of this element is that the temptation to fit more in is overwhelming, and many site owners and designers succumb to the desire to put everything they can on the homepage. Oftentimes, this just becomes bloat, but at other times, it can be an elegant way to present more content in a slide show style.

One of the upsides to using this approach is that instead of a long page to scroll down, the user can absorb the information one chunk at a time. This also gives the designer the ability to tell a story, as they have greater control over the order you view content.

The Emotech site (Figure 1) demonstrates a pretty standard approach to this style. The large banner at the top (including the image and text) slides side to side between frames. It has arrows on either side, indicating that you can move forward or backward through the frames. This is what you might call the standard approach to slide shows.

A less traditional example would be the Kodu homepage (Figure 3). In this case, the slide show is not confined to the standard rectangle. Instead, it includes the image of an iPhone, which overlaps the header of the page. The transition is basically a fade in and fade out style; instead of arrows, it has three dots to represent the different stages and to allow for manually jumping to the desired frame.

Another creative solution that demonstrates how a slightly tweaked standard can feel fresh and new is the Cubicle Ninjas homepage slide show (Figure 2). Two things make this one stand out. First of all, it is entirely user driven. It doesn't just rotate while you're idle—you have to interact with it and take the next step. Second, there is no indication that this is a slide show at all. The first time I clicked the button on the site, I thought I would get a new page. Instead, it slid over to the next frame. These subtle changes maintain usability while adapting to the specific needs of the site.

Figure 1 http://www.emotech.com.au

Figure 2 http://cubicleninjas.com

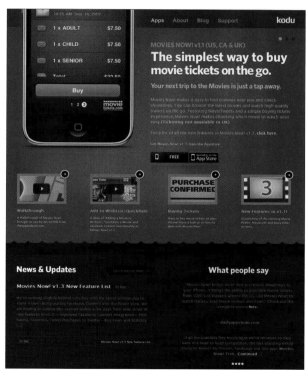

Figure 3 http://www.kodu.co.uk

http://www.steveprezant.com

http://www.interdevil.com

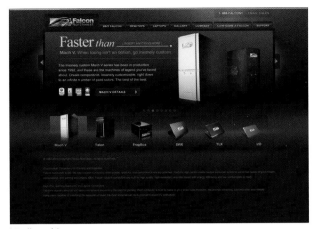

http://www.falcon-nw.com

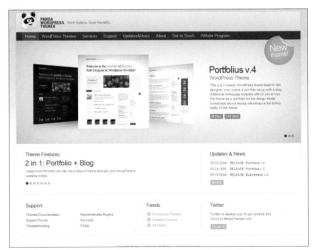

http://pandathemes.com

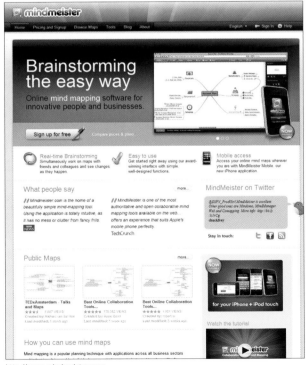

http://www.mindmeister.com

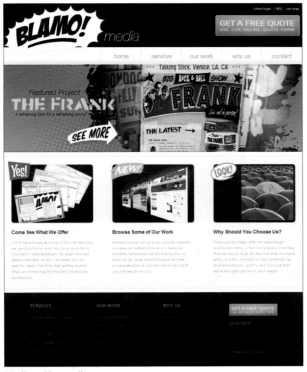

http://www.blamomedia.ca

notes from a developer

If you're looking to have a slick little slide show on a page, chances are you will be looking into various JavaScript-based solutions. In particular, you should check out one of the countless jQuery-based slide shows in their plug-in library (http://plugins.jquery.com); jQuery makes amazing things possible.

If you're tempted to do something that involves more advanced transitions or text effects, you're going to be looking at creating a Flash movie. This isn't a problem, it's just a very different skill set, and it tends to take a lot more time. So keep this in mind as you consider your budget and the impact your design has on the overall cost of the project. Using a much simpler JavaScript-based solution is a very cost effective way to get the desired functionality without sinking the budget.

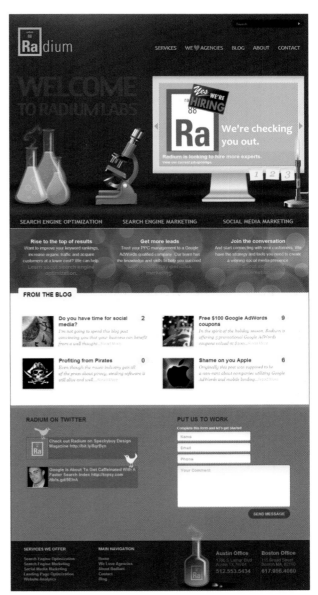

http://www.radiumlabs.com

http://www.fmair.com

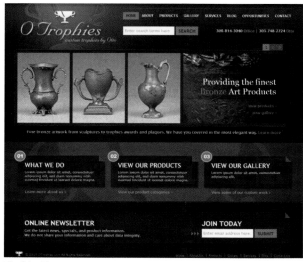

http://otrophies.com

http://www.elevationchurch.org

http://www.treemolabs.com

http://divita.eu

http://www.nevilledesign.com

404 pages

The 404 page is most likely the last thing on a designer's mind when creating web design concepts, and most developers (including me) neglect to include it. The sites referenced here are notable not only because they bothered to create a 404 page, but also because they made them into something useful, beautiful and, at times, funny.

The design of the Carsonified 404 page (Figure 1) integrates perfectly with the site and is easy on the eyes. More importantly, the page provides the user with key links to point him in the right direction. This takes an otherwise lost opportunity and does its best to salvage the situation.

The Studio Weber 404 page takes a different approach (Figure 2). Here, they kindly inform you that you landed on a dead page, but rather than simply redirect you somewhere else, they actually filled the page with content and functionality. I would speculate that this is the most sought-after content, and certainly represents what the site owner wants to present to the user. This is what I call maximizing your results!

The Graphik 404 page (Figure 3) does something slightly different (and fairly common)—it suggests that you head over to the homepage and start from scratch. Not a bad idea, when you think about it. However the user ended up on the page, he is likely to want to reboot his approach to the site. This is an especially good approach with a site that isn't heavy on content, as the error page will likely just reflect the home page anyway.

http://www.fhoke.com

Figure 1 http://www.carsonified.com

http://www.ndesign-studio.com

http://www.monolinea.com

Figure 2 http://www.studioweber.com

Figure 3 http://graphik.fi

http://www.tylergaw.com

http://www.shayhowe.com

http://www.pixelthread.co.uk

http://www.dockerydesign.com

index/permissions

p. 028 http://www.fontex.org Rade Joksimovic © 2009

p. 028 http://www.wilsondoors.com Openfield Creative © 2009

p. 028 http://www.gcntv.org Global Christian Network © 2009

p. 028 http://www.recaper.com Mubashar Iqbal © 2009

p. 029 http://www.sofiaregalo.com Sofia Regalo © 2009

p. 029 http://garyplayer.com Paramore|Redd © 2009

p. 029 http://hungryhowies.com © 2009 TargetScope Inc.

p. 029 http://www.digitalnoon.com Nick Kutateli © 2009

p. 031 http://libertyboom.com © 2009 Magnate Interactive

p. 032 http://tearoundapp.com We Collaborate / Crafty Corp © 2009

p. 032 http://www.ticatacgames.net/static/iphone_teaser Treemo Labs © 2009

p. 032 http://www.outpostapp.com David Kaneda © 2009

p. 032 http://www.glasshouse-apps.com Glasshouse Apps © 2009

p. 033 http://syphone.selcukyilmaz.com selcuk yilmaz © 2009

p. 033 http://skimaps.planetreesoftware.com Lennart Schoors © 2010

p. 034 http://www.baristaapp.com Glasshouse Apps © 2009

p. 034 http://www.momentoapp.com d3i © 2009

p. 034 http://www.2udoku.com Toopia © 2009

p. 035 http://www.thermometerapp.com Toopia © 2009

p. 035 http://www.futuretap.com/home/whereto-en FutureTap © 2009

p. 035 http://tapbots.com/weightbot Tapbots, LLC © 2009

p. 037 http://www.digitalmash.com Rob Morris © 2009

p. 037 http://www.djgd.co.uk David James © 2009

p. 037 http://www.traxor-designs.com Traxor Designs © 2010

p. 037 http://www.ronniesan.com © 2009 by Ronnie Garcia

p. 038 http://www.patrickmonkel.nl Monk Design © 2009

p. 038 http://madebyelephant.com Tim Van Damme © 2009

p. 038 http://www.lynncyr.com Lynn Cyr © 1996-2010

p. 039 http://www.zivmeltzer.com Ziv Meltzer © 2009

p. 039 http://www.brizk.com Kai Brach © 2009

p. 040 http://petehellyer.com Pete Hellyer © 2009

p. 040 http://larkef.com Larkef © 2009

p. 040 http://ryanplesko.com Ryan Plesko © 2009

p. 041 http://betterplacerecordings.com Elliot Jay Stocks © 2009

p. 042 http://www.goodbyeelliott.com Dan Behrens © 2009

p. 042 http://www.standardthompson.com Dan Behrens © 2009

p. 042 http://www.theiveysmusic.com Darcy Fray © 2009

p. 043 http://www.rocketclub.info Dan Behrens © 2009

p. 043 http://www.dimmn.com Dan Behrens © 2009

p. 043 http://10outoftenn.com Otterball © 2009

p. 043 http://www.jazzforme.de Marco Rullkoetter AGD © 2009

p. 044 http://www.sickcityclub.net Zaum & Brown © 2009

p. 044 http://www.muddriverunion.com/index.htm hitcents.com © 2009

p. 044 http://sourhaze.com/ep1 Elliot Jay Stocks © 2009

p. 044 http://www.marianastrench.net Marianas Trench © 2009

p. 045 http://www.inspiredm.com Inspired Magazine © 2009

p. 046 http://www.designshard.com Max Stanworth © 2009

p. 046 http://www.theoldstate.com/blog The Old State LLC © 2009

p. 047 http://www.idsgn.org idsgn © 2009

p. 047 http://upsidestudio.com J. David Link © 2009

p. 048 http://snook.ca Jonathan Snook © 2009

p. 048 http://razvanphotography.com Razvan Horeanga © 2009

p. 048 http://www.havocinspired.co.uk Copyright © 2009 - Havoc Inspired - Ryan Taylor

p. 049 http://jasonsantamaria.com Jason Santa Maria © 2001-2009

p. 049 http://beyondjazz.net Lennart Schoors © 2009

p. 050 http://blog.cocoia.com Cocoia © 2009

p. 050 http://exp.horizontal.mykl.nl © 2009 Maykel Loomans. All Rights Reserved.

p. 050 http://roquealonso.org Roque Alonso © 2008-2009

p. 051 http://www.havocinspired.co.uk Ryan Taylor © 2009

p. 052 http://chrissloan.info Chris Sloan © 2009

p. 052 http://www.jasongraphix.com Jason Beaird © 2009

p. 052 http://www.chiappisi.com Fourth Floor Interactive © 2009

p. 052 http://www.joedowdle.com Otterball © 2009

p. 053 http://benjaminminnich.com BenjaminMinnich© 2009

p. 053 http://www.liamjmoore.com Liam J Moore © 2009

p. 053 http://www.neboo5.net Branko Sabaric © 2009

p. 054 http://www.tjmapes.com TJ Mapes © 2009

p. 054 http://www.allaboutchris.co.uk Chris Lowry © 2009

p. 055 http://komodomedia.com Rogie King © 2009

p. 056 http://www.thisisgrow.com Grow Interactive © 2009

p. 056 http://www.saizenmedia.com Saizen Media Studios © 2009

p. 056 http://www.syck.com Syck © 2009

p. 056 http://paramoreredd.com Paramore|Redd © 2009

p. 056 http://www.aspect-webdesign.com Aspect-Webdesign © 2009

p. 057 http://www.24-7media.de 247mediastudios © 2009

p. 057 http://definecreative.com.au Define Creative © 2009

p. 057 http://madebyrocket.com © rocket 2009

p. 057 http://www.zaum.co.uk Zaum & Brown © 2009

p. 058 http://www.thinkcw.com C+W © 2009

p. 058 **http://www.area17.com** AREA?17 © 2009

p. 058 **http://www.periscope.com** PERISCOPE © 2009

p. 058 **http://junecloud.com** © 2009 Junecloud LLC

p. 059 **http://www.randolphfair.com** IBG Design Group © 2009

p. 060 **http://www.uabama.com/lectures** UAB I AMA © 2009

p. 060 **http://www.doyoupk.org** Openfield Creative © 2009

p. 060 **http://www.festivalboreal.com** Jorge Mesa © 2009

p. 060 **http://blogsville.us** Jesse Friedman © 2009

p. 060 **http://www.therustyball.com** Openfield Creative © 2009

p. 061 **http://summercamp.carsonified.com** Carsonified © 2009

p. 061 **http://naias.com** Openfield Creative © 2009

p. 062 **http://www.reelrocktour.com** branodn todd wilson © 2009

p. 062 **http://www.visitsalford.info/foodfestival** Dave Cunningham © 2009

p. 062 **http://stackoverflow.carsonified.com** Carsonified © 2009

p. 064 **http://www.welcometobricktown.com** Funnel Design Group © 2009

p. 064 **http://www.gatesopen.ca** Lucky Cat Design © 2009

p. 064 **http://www.sani-resort.com** Sani Resorts © 2009

p. 065 **http://www.definitelydubai.com** Dubai Tourism & Xische Studios © 2009

p. 065 **http://www.campingilfrutteto.it** il Frutteto © 2009

p. 065 **http://www.amsterdam-bed-and-break-fasts.com** Amsterdam Bed and Breakfasts © 2009

p. 066 **http://treasureislandcasino.com** PERISCOPE © 2009

p. 066 **http://www.trappfamily.com** Trapp Family Lodge I Tag New Media © 2009

p. 066 **http://www.paristaylorhotel.com** Notio Web Design © 2009

p. 066 **http://www.barceloraval.com** Barcelo © 2009

p. 066 **http://www.icystraitpoint.com** G Lamson © 2009

p. 068 **http://www.asphaltgold.de** asphaltgold sneakerstore © 2009

p. 068 **http://www.readyhang.com** ReadyHang.com © 2009. Design: UD+M, uberdm.com

p. 068 **http://www.yayadog.com** yayadog © 2009

p. 068 **http://www.letscollect.co.uk** James Stewart www.letscollect.co.uk © 2009

p. 069 **http://www.threadless.com** © 2010, Threadless, a skinnyCorp LLC company. All designs copyright by owner.

p. 069 **http://www.onetribe.com** OneTribe © 2009

p. 070 **http://www.twelvesouth.com** © 2009 Twelve South LLC

p. 070 **http://ridefourever.com** brandon todd wilson © 2009

p. 070 **http://www.creativesoutfitter.com** Behance, LLC © 2009

p. 071 **http://www.teapot.cl** Andrea Pérez Dalannays © 2009

p. 071 **http://www.uniqlo.co.uk** Uniqlo © 2009

p. 071 **http://jaqkcellars.com** JAQK Cellars © 2009

p. 071 **http://www.matthewwilliamson.com** Matthew Williamson © 2009

p. 072 **http://www.leandaryan.com** Leanda Ryan © 2009

p. 072 **http://www.jonwardweb.co.uk** jonwardweb © 2009

p. 073 **http://timvandamme.com** Tim Van Damme © 2009

p. 073 **http://waqasashraf.com** Waqas Ashraf © 2009

p. 073 **http://www.ultimate-mediagroup.nl** ultimate media group © 2009

p. 073 **http://appenstein.com** Appenstein, LLC © 2009

p. 073 **http://www.jordankeating.com** jordankeating © 2009

p. 073 **http://andycroll.com** Andy Croll © 2009

p. 074 **http://brisdom.com/evertslagter** Evert Slagter © 2009

p. 074 **http://rogieking.com** Rogie King © 2009

p. 074 **http://bitminers.com** BitMiners LLC © 2009

p. 075 **http://thurlyapp.com** elixirgraphics © 2009

p. 076 **http://www.sonarhq.com** Boost Ltd © 2009

p. 076 **http://www.w3roi.com** Awio Web Services LLC © 2009

p. 076 **http://ceevee.com** CeeVee © 2009

p. 076 **http://shortwaveapp.com** Shaun Inman © 2009

p. 077 **http://www.stayvalid.com** nickhand.net © 2009

p. 077 **http://heywatch.com** Particles © 2009

p. 077 **http://wufoo.com** Infinity Box Inc. © 2009

p. 077 **http://www.buzzsprout.com** Molehill © 2009

p. 079 **http://www.kartel.co.nz** Boost Ltd © 2009

p. 079 **http://www.campaignmonitor.com** Campaign Monitor © 2009

p. 079 **http://lemonstandapp.com** Limewheel Creative Inc. © 2009

p. 079 **http://www.notableapp.com** ZURB © 2009

p. 080 **http://invoicemachine.com** Bombia Design AB © 2009

p. 080 **http://feedafever.com** Shaun Inman © 2009

p. 081 **http://www.cubescripts.com** copyright by CubeScripts.com

p. 081 **http://www.easytasker.com** LB Digital © 2009

p. 082 **http://www.interactive-business.com.au** MBG Interactive © 2010

p. 082 **http://www.splash360.com** Splash360 Incorporated © 2009

p. 084 **http://www.lifesabounce.com** WeLove72 © 2009

p. 084 **http://www.cphomesatarchersrock.com** CP Homes at Archers Rock © 2009

p. 084 **http://www.provincewest.com** SiteWave.Com © 2009

p. 084 **http://www.championllc.com** G Lamson © 2009

p. 085 **http://www.bornliving.com** Miguel Ripoll (www.miguelripoll.com) © 2009

p. 085 **http://www.hillwoodresidential.com** Concussion Interactive © 2009

p. 085 **http://breedenhomes.com** Origen Creatives © 2009

p. 085 **http://www.chrisfenemore.com** Chris Fenemore © 2009

p. 086 **http://www.jprealtyservices.com** JP Realty Services © 2009

p. 086 **http://www.alghadeer.ae** © 2009 Sorouh

p. 086 **http://www.mpwproperties.com** G Lamson © 2009

p. 088 http://www.brianhoff.net Brian Hoff / TDC Brand © 2009

p. 088 http://www.ruyadorno.com Ruy Adorno

p. 088 http://www.markdearman.com Mark Dearman © 2009

p. 088 http://www.dosbros.nl ruud puylaert @ 2009

p. 089 http://www.toby-powell.co.uk Toby Powell © 2009

p. 089 http://www.susiemcconnell.com Susie McConnell © 2009

p. 090 http://www.pyttel.sk Roman Pittner © 2009

p. 090 http://two24studios.com Jason Walker © 2009

p. 090 http://www.yodabaz.com Basile Tournier © 2009

p. 090 http://www.shadddales.com Shadd Dales © 2009

p. 091 http://www.alexcohaniuc.com Alex Cohaniuc © 2009

p. 091 http://www.danieloliver.co.uk Daniel Oliver © 2009

p. 091 http://sjhunter.net Adam Lloyd © 2009

p. 091 http://www.ermanerkur.com Erman Erkur © 2009

p. 092 http://www.firenetworks.com FireHost © 2009

p. 092 http://www.fireexchange.com FireHost © 2009

p. 093 http://www.syrrup.com Jennifer Yen © 2009

p. 093 http://www.solidshops.com Joris Hens / Dries Droesbeke © 2009

p. 093 http://www.lukesbeard.com Lukesbeard © 2009

p. 093 http://www.upstatedesign.org Tyler Finck © 2009

p. 094 http://www.freshdeals.com Fresh Deals © 2009

p. 094 http://www.branchesdesign.co.uk Branches Design © 2009

p. 094 http://www.shortinc.com Abuse the System, Inc. © 2009

p. 095 http://birdboxx.com © 2009 birdboxmedia. com & idokungfoo.com

p. 095 http://wordpress-workshops.com WordPress Workshops © 2009

p. 095 http://squidchef.com Piotr Godek © 2009

p. 095 http://www.formmule.com Formmule © 2009

p. 096 http://www.wuwi.com Bindoff Media © 2010

p. 097 http://www.yellowbirdproject.com www.goDynamo.com © 2009

p. 097 http://www.unrealcotton.com INSPIRE Creative Solutions © 2009

p. 097 http://www.cosmicsoda.com CosmicSoda © 2009

p. 098 http://www.milkandeggsco.com Milk and Eggs Co. © 2009

p. 098 https://www.drippinginfat.com WeLove72 © 2009

p. 098 http://www.ittybittee.com Ittybittee © 2009

p. 098 http://www.gotmojo.co.uk GotMojo © 2008

p. 099 http://www.riptapparel.com TJ Mapes © 2009

p. 099 http://200nipples.com Tiny Sauce, LLC © 2009

p. 100 http://www.patriciaferreira.com Patrícia Ferreira © 2009

p. 101 http://www.storenvy.com Storenvy © 2010

p. 101 http://www.aroundme.com Integrity © 2009

p. 102 http://www.theuxbookmark.com Abhay Rautela © 2009

p. 102 http://www.practicelink.com Integrity © 2009

p. 102 http://www.freshdeals.com Fresh Deals © 2009

p. 105 http://www.conceptfeedback.com Concept Feedback LLC © 2009

p. 105 http://www.periscopecreative.com Periscope Creative © 2009

p. 105 http://www.patrickmonkel.nl Monk Design © 2009

p. 105 http://kindredspiritstn.org Brad Haynes © 2009

p. 106 http://rawkes.com Rob Hawkes © 2009

p. 106 http://www.antidecaf.com Anders Johnsen © 2009

p. 106 http://www.performanceedgepartners.com © 2009 FireHost Inc.

p. 106 http://www.smalldotstudios.com © Copyright 2009 Small Dot Studios

p. 107 http://www.design-manchester.co.uk David Rushton © 2009

p. 107 http://www.arcticcat.com/snow PERISCOPE © 2009

p. 108 http://www.studiow.com.my Studio W © 2009

p. 108 http://wtmworldwide.com © 2010

p. 108 http://www.skrotskystudio.com Vadim Skrotsky Studio © 2009

p. 108 http://www.reinvigorate.net Reinvigorate © 2010

p. 109 http://ryanmcmaster.com Ryan McMaster © 2009

p. 110 http://strutta.com Strutta Media, Inc. © 2009

p. 110 http://trystentertainment.com Marie Bushbaum © 2009

p. 110 http://www.pizzainn.com © 2009 TargetScope Inc.

p. 110 http://www.zionseven.net zionseven.net © 2009

p. 111 http://neutroncreations.com Tim Van Damme © 2009

p. 111 http://www.digitalgurus.co.uk WeLove72 © 2009

p. 111 http://tomatogallery.yzx.se Martin Ahlberger © 2009

p. 111 http://www.addnoise.nl Add Noise Internet & Design © 2009

p. 112 http://www.mdxinteractive.com MDX Interactive, LLC © 2009

p. 112 http://www.factoria.me Factoría Crossmedia © 2009

p. 113 http://cannonballcommunications.com Enso © 2009

p. 113 http://adcapitalindustries.com Logistetica © 2008

p. 113 http://www.harlandwilliams.com Harland Williams © 2009

p. 113 http://kissmetrics.com KISSmetrics © 2009

p. 114 http://www.gelattina.com Gelattina.com © 2009

p. 115 http://arat.cz Lukás Foldýna © 2009

p. 115 http://www.bottlerocketapps.com Bottle Rocket Apps © 2009

p. 115 http://www.cellar-app.com Glasshouse Apps © 2009

p. 116 http://icedcocoa.com Louis Harboe © 2009

p. 116 **http://www.imagemakers.uk.com** Imagemakers © 2009

p. 117 **http://www.liftux.com** Walmedia, LLC dba Lift © 2009

p. 117 **http://www.magnateinteractive.com** © 2009 Magnate Interactive

p. 117 **http://www.cinemobits.com.br** mobits © 2009

p. 117 **http://www.mockdraftapp.com** Tap Tapas © 2009

p. 118 **http://www.flipside5.com** FlipSide5, Inc. © 2008-2009

p. 118 **http://www.rovingbird.com/touringmobilis-nl** SHpartners bvba © 2009

p. 119 **http://www.albertlo.com** Albert Lo © 2009

p. 120 **http://www.kimburgess.info** Kim Burgess © 2009

p. 120 **http://maustingraphics.com** Michael Austin © 2009

p. 120 **http://www.lisabun.com** Lisa Bun © 2009

p. 120 **http://www.aus120.com** Design120 © 2009

p. 121 **http://www.johnphillips.me** John Phillips © 2009

p. 121 **http://adellecharles.com** Adelle Charles © 2010

p. 121 **http://www.cucweb.org** Chomolungma UNESCO Centre © 2009

p. 122 **http://www.visualgroove.net** Febby Tan © 2009

p. 122 **http://3diddi.com** dnna © 2009

p. 122 **http://www.kmkzband.com** Sterovisualdesign.p. com © 2009

p. 122 **http://www.levikoi.com** LeviKoi c 2009

p. 124 **http://53mondays.com** Lesly Garreau © 2009

p. 124 **http://vip.grooveshark.com** Escape Media Group © 2009

p. 124 **http://www.thepeachdesign.com** © 2010 THE PEACH DESIGN. ALL RIGHTS RESERVED.

p. 125 **http://www.id83.nl** Lieve Sonke © 2009

p. 125 **http://theiconlab.com** elixir graphics © 2006-2009

p. 125 **http://getconcentrating.com** © rocket 2009

p. 126 **http://www.gositewave.com** SiteWave.Com © 2009

p. 126 **http://www.jp3design.com** Jason Peters, JP3 DESIGN © 2010

p. 126 **http://www.ebandlive.com** eBandLive © 2010

p. 126 **http://nmiciano.com** Noel Miciano © 2009

p. 127 **http://www.easyink.com.au** SimpleFlame © 2010

p. 127 **http://www.southernmedia.net** Southern Media © 2009

p. 127 **http://velthy.net** Stefan Velthuys © 2009

p. 128 **http://www.topazti.com** TOPAZ Technologies © 2009

p. 128 **http://www.shape5.com** Shape 5 LLC © 2009

p. 129 **http://jbradforddillon.com** J. Bradford Dillon © 2010

p. 130 **http://www.darrenhoyt.com** Darren Hoyt © 2009

p. 130 **http://thecodesign.org** Ryan Plesko © 2009

p. 130 **http://beargraphics.co.uk** David Emery © 2009

p. 131 **http://www.behoff.com** Brian Hoff Design, LLC © 2010

p. 131 **http://ligatureloopandstem.com** Ligature, Loop & Stem © 2009

p. 132 **http://www.typechart.com** Panduka Senaka © 2009

p. 132 **http://www.thevileplutocrat.com** 16toads Design © 2009

p. 133 **http://www.integritystl.com** Integrity © 2009

p. 133 **http://www.squarefour.net** squarefour © 2009

p. 133 **http://www.piscataqua.com/index.aspx** Piscataqua Savings Bank © 2010

p. 133 **http://www.lovefreelancing.com** Kai Brach © 2009

p. 134 **http://malwin-faber.de** Malwin Faber © 2009

p. 134 **http://www.votedougducey.com/** FireHost Inc. © 2010

p. 135 **http://www.bensky.co.uk** Ben Sky © 2009

p. 136 **http://www.thisisleaf.co.uk** SB Studio © 2009

p. 136 **http://blog.newsok.com/afghanistan-iraq/mikes-blog** Kristopher Kanaly © 2009

p. 136 **http://www.housetopmedia.com** Church Plant Media © 2010

p. 136 **http://www.njwebdesign.co.za** The Creative Dot © 2009

p. 137 **http://www.rommil.com** Rommil Santiago © 2009

p. 137 **http://www.noahshrader.com** Noah Shrader © 2009

p. 137 **http://www.davyknowles.com** Satsu Limited © 2009

p. 137 **http://www.albus.fi** Aleksi Partanen © 2009

p. 138 **http://www.superieur-graphique.com** Sven Stüber for Superieur Graphique © 2009

p. 138 **http://v1.maykelloomans.com** © 1985 - 2009 Maykel Loomans. All Rights Reserved

p. 138 **http://www.schlossanger.de** Schlossanger Alp GmbH Co. Kg. © 2009

p. 138 **http://www.dettaglio.co.uk** We Love... © 2009

p. 138 **http://www.lightqube.co.uk** We Love... © 2009

p. 140 **http://www.brianhoff.net** Brian Hoff Design, LLC © 2010

p. 141 **http://www.nosotroshq.com** Juanma Teixido © 2009

p. 141 **http://www.nanointegris.com** Twist Systems Ltd © 2009

p. 141 **http://eighty8four.com** Eighty8Four, Inc © 2009

p. 142 **http://www.jamiegregory.co.uk** Jamie Gregory © 2010

p. 142 **http://kiwithemes.com** Elixir Graphics © 2009

p. 142 **http://nihongoup.com** Philip Seyfi © 2009

p. 142 **http://fusionads.net** Elliot Jay Stocks © 2009

p. 143 **http://www.rihardsonline.com** Rihards Steinbergs © 2009

p. 143 **http://www.prothemedesign.com** Pro Theme Design © 2009

p. 143 **http://www.hotgloo.com** HotGloo © 2009

p. 143 **http://www.admkids.com** PERISCOPE © 2009

p. 144 **http://www.paperrep.com** Central National-Gottesman Inc. © 2009

p. 144 **http://www.pixelflips.com** Phillip Lovelace © 2009

p. 144 **http://www.superuserstudio.com** Super User Studio © 2010

p. 146 **http://www.inboxaward.com** © INBOX AWARD

p. 146 **http://www.sreski.com** Mark Dormand © 2009

p. 146 **http://www.retrostrobe.com** retrostrobe* © 2009

p. 146 **http://nathancarnes.com** Nathan Carnes © 2009

p. 147 **http://www.pfxcontracts.net** PFX Contracts Ltd © 2009

p. 147 **http://www.conetrees.com** Cone Trees © 2009

p. 147 **http://www.fourthfloorinteractive.com** Fourth Floor Interactive © 2009

p. 147 **http://robertsonuk.net** © 2009 robertsonuk.net

p. 148 **http://www.studiozfilms.com** Studio+Z Films © 2010

p. 148 **http://www.ryanjclose.com** Ryan Close © 2009

p. 148 **http://www.playout.pt** Playout © 2009 · PLAYOUT.PT

p. 148 **http://plsr.net** Jan Hendrik Weiss © 2009

p. 149 **http://www.airbnb.com** Airbnb, Inc © 2009

p. 149 **http://lensco.be** Lennart Schoors © 2009

p. 149 **http://www.diografic.com** Diografic© 2009

p. 149 **http://www.rozner.pl** Jacek Rozner © 2009

p. 151 **http://twiggy.carsonified.com** Carsonified © 2009

p. 151 **http://www.crayonslife.com** Jesusa Ayala Dayate © 2009

p. 151 **http://www.camellie.com** camellie © 2009

p. 151 **http://www.happyingreenville.com** Bon Secours St. Francis Health System © 2009

p. 151 **http://ami.wookypooky.com** Amelia Chen © 2009

p. 152 **http://www.tylergaw.com** Tyler Gaw © 2009

p. 152 **http://www.rawcoach.be** Lennart Schoors © 2009

p. 152 **http://mesonprojekt.com** Karl Francisco Fernandes © 2009

p. 153 **http://www.albertocerriteno.com** Alberto Cerriteno © 2009

p. 153 **http://www.espiratecnologias.com** Espira © 2009

p. 153 **http://www.chrisspooner.com** Chris Spooner © 2009

p. 153 **http://www.ebandlive.com/users/dirtydozenbrassband803** eBandLive © 2010

p. 155 **http://real-sangria.com** Cread an MGSCOMM Company© 2009

p. 155 **http://www.Duirwaigh.com** Angi Sullins & Silas Toball, Duirwaigh, Inc. © 2009

p. 155 **http://www.adamsmagic.com** Adam Cope © 2009

p. 155 **http://www.mattnortham.com** Matt Northam © 2009

p. 156 **http://www.signshopmarketing.com** Graphic D-Signs, Inc. © 2009

p. 156 **http://chirp.twitter.com** Twitter © 2009

p. 156 **http://www.carbonsugar.com** Design120 © 2009

p. 157 **http://www.bbc.co.uk/cbbc/tracybeaker** BBC © 2009

p. 157 **http://bigskynj.com** Big Sky Associates, LLC. © 2009

p. 157 **http://arose.biz** A.R.O.S.E. © 2009

p. 158 **http://www.comfortbrothers.com** Comfort Brothers © 2009

p. 158 **http://zionsnowboards.com** brandon todd wilson © 2009

p. 159 **http://blog.spoongraphics.co.uk** Chris Spooner © 2009

p. 159 **http://www.joaozanatta.com.br** joaozanatta © 2009

p. 159 **http://www.swimmingwithbabies.com** Madhu Sharma © 2009

p. 160 **http://www.francescomugnai.com** FrancescoMugnai.com © 2009

p. 161 **http://www.firehost.com** © 2009 FireHost Inc.

p. 161 **http://www.edelwwweiss.com** Delphine Pagès © 2009

p. 161 **http://www.lionite.com** lionite © 2009

p. 161 **http://www.launchmind.com** LaunchMind Ltd © 2009

p. 162 **http://www.emergence-day.com** Saizen Media Studios © 2009

p. 162 **http://kiwi-app.net** YourHead Software © 2009

p. 162 **http://insectropolis.com** Insectropolis © 2009

p. 163 **http://www.saizenmedia.com/FFIV** Saizen Media Studios © 2009

p. 163 **http://www.saizenmedia.com/nightwish** Saizen Media Studios © 2009

p. 163 **http://shauninman.com** Shaun Inman © 2009

p. 163 **http://www.cupcakecarousel.co.uk** cupcakecarousel © 2009

p. 163 **http://culturapositiva.com** Social Snack © 2009

p. 164 **http://tomatic.com** Thomas Marban © 2009

p. 164 **http://www.sunskool.com** Storm Sustainability © 2009

p. 164 **http://events.carsonified.com** Carsonified © 2009

p. 164 **http://www.mikimottes.com** Miki Mottes © 2009

p. 165 **http://www.amitkhera.com** www.amitkhera.com © 2009

p. 165 **http://www.2pitch.com** 2pitch © 2009

p. 166 **http://www.endemit.si** david praznik © 2009

p. 167 **http://www.shayhowe.com** Shay Howe © 2009

p. 167 **http://www.miguelbuckenmeyer.com** Miguel Buckenmeyer © 2009

p. 167 **http://dj.johnyfavourite.co.uk** Favourite Media © 2009

p. 167 **http://www.wedesignwise.com** Designwise © 2010

p. 168 **http://www.nkbookreviews.com** Nate Klaiber © 2009

p. 168 **http://www.min-style.de** Jann de Vries © 2009

p. 169 **http://www.unieq.nl** Dirk Leys © 2009

p. 169 **http://www.gesteves.com** Guillermo Esteves © 2009

p. 169 **http://m1k3.net** Michael Dick © 2010

p. 169 **http://www.leandaryan.com** Leanda Ryan © 2009

p. 170 **http://www.brandedcode.com** Micheil Smith © 2009

p. 170 **http://www.syrrup.com** Jennifer Yen © 2009

p. 170 **http://de-online.co.uk** David Emery © 2010

p. 170 **http://www.sabeapp.com** Cubedroute © 2009

p. 171 **http://www.theglasgowcollective.com** BigWaveDesign © 2009

p. 172 **http://www.remixcreative.net** Nik Gill © 2009

p. 172 **http://www.alingham.com** Al Ingham © 2010

p. 172 **http://www.intuitionhq.com** Boost New Media © 2009

p. 172 **http://www.helveticbrands.ch** David Pache © 2010

p. 173 **http://the99percent.com** Behance, LLC © 2009

p. 202 http://www.rdbrown.me.uk Richard Brown © 2009

p. 202 http://www.digitalic.org/portfolio Digitalic © 2009

p. 202 http://www.tmsportmanagement.com TM Sportmanagement © 2009

p. 202 http://www.xische.com Xische Studios & Danish Farhan © 2009

p. 203 http://f91w.com Neil Scott © 2010

p. 203 http://www.finalcutters.com Digital Heaven Ltd © 2010

p. 203 http://www.lyricalmedia.com John O'Nolan © 2009

p. 203 http://www.nvlstudio.com Aleksi Partanen © 2009

p. 204 http://www.soeppainting.com Lightfin Studios © 2009

p. 204 http://www.classicsapp.com Andrew Kaz & Phill Ryu © 2009

p. 204 http://www.rabbleandrouser.com rabble+rouser, inc © 2008

p. 204 http://designspasm.net Sean Geng © 2009

p. 206 http://www.siebennull.com Marc Hinse I siebennull.com © 2009

p. 206 http://www.tuckinteractiv.com tuckinteractiv © 2009

p. 206 http://www.floridaflourish.com © 2010 Flourish Web Design

p. 206 http://eyedraw.eu Piotr Godek © 2009

p. 207 http://www.ladeq.it LADEQ © 2009

p. 207 http://www.howarths.nl WeLove72 © 2009

p. 207 http://www.joshsmithdesign.com Josh Smith © 2008

p. 208 http://www.seankeenan.org.uk Sean Keenan © 2009

p. 208 http://meetjohnvon.com John P Gelety © 2009

p. 208 http://www.gavincastleton.com Tyler Finck © 2009

p. 209 http://www.johnantoni.com John Griffiths © 2009

p. 209 http://www.sursly.com Tyler Finck © 2009

p. 209 http://www.alexarts.ru/en Alexey Abramov © 2009

p. 209 http://www.chameleon-home.com PLUSX.de © 2009

p. 211 http://www.vanityclaire.com F. Claire Baxter © 2009

p. 211 http://www.melissamariehernandez.com Justin Lerner © 2009

p. 211 http://cyberwoven.com Cyberwoven © 2009

p. 212 http://www.pinchotforest.com Integritive © 2009

p. 212 http://www.hasrimy.com hasrimy.com © 2009

p. 213 http://www.avilasoto.com avilasoto © 2009

p. 213 http://album.alexflueras.ro Alex Flueras © 2009

p. 215 http://oldergraphicdesigner.com Older Graphic Designer © Jack Bloom 2009

p. 215 http://www.kaabstudios.com KAAB © 2010

p. 215 http://www.nineflavors.com NineFlavors.com © 2009

p. 215 http://samanthacliffe.com Samantha Cliffe & Elliot Jay Stocks © 2009

p. 216 http://socialsnack.com Social Snack © 2009

p. 216 http://www.holtedesign.no Holte Design © 2009

p. 217 http://www.contrabrand.net brandon todd wilson © 2009

p. 217 http://www.draftmedia.de Thomas Schröpfer © 2009

p. 217 http://www.brian-eagan.com Brian Eagan © 2009

p. 217 http://lancamjewellery.co.uk © 2009 robertsonuk.net

p. 218 http://pixelmanya.com Dominik Mertz © 2009

p. 218 http://www.thismortalmagic.com Jan Pautsch.Lilienthal © 2009

p. 218 http://byroxanne.com Roxanne Labajo © 2009

p. 219 http://www.ultimate-media.nl ultimate media group © 2009

p. 219 http://www.brizk.com Kai Brach © 2009

p. 219 http://www.fajnechlopaki.com Fajne chlopaki © 2009

p. 219 http://www.gnoso.com Gnoso Inc © 2009

p. 221 http://quirkylotus.com quirkylotus © 2009

p. 222 http://www.clothmoth.com Ryan Foster © 2009

p. 222 http://www.narfstuff.co.uk/portfolio Fran Boot © 2009

p. 222 http://thecssblog.com Ignacio Ricci © 2009

p. 223 http://www.imdesignuk.com imdesign © 2009

p. 223 http://www.msites.com Molehill © 2009

p. 223 http://www.metalabdesign.com MetaLab Design Ltd © 2009

p. 223 http://www.piensaenpixels.com Jimena Catalina Gayo © 2009

p. 224 http://www.manisheriar.com Sheriar Designs © 2009

p. 225 http://www.ascendsport.com MG Nutritionals Pty Ltd © 2009

p. 225 http://www.nanastreak.com/webdesignersidea/eBandLive eBandLive © 2009

p. 226 http://www.airbnb.com Airbnb, Inc © 2009

p. 226 http://www.notableapp.com ZURB © 2009

p. 226 http://www.gofreelance.org Kai Brach © 2009

p. 226 http://www.serj.ca Serj Kozlov © 2009

p. 227 http://www.mailchimp.com Copyright © 2009 MailChimp

p. 227 http://theimagescanners.com SimpleFlame © 2010

p. 227 http://www.ncover.com Gnoso Inc. © 2009

p. 227 http://www.sonarhq.com Boost Ltd © 2009

p. 228 http://www.uploadpie.com Upload Pie © 2009

p. 228 http://www.jamiebicknell.com Jamie Bicknell © 2009

p. 228 http://www.storenvy.com Storenvy © 2010

p. 228 http://www.1stchoiceaccommodations.com FireHost Inc. © 2010

p. 228 http://www.classicplanestv.com © 2009 HigherSites

p. 230 http://guified.com GUIFIED © 2009

p. 230 http://www.traditionalboundaries.com Deep Blue Sky © 2009

p. 230 http://www.kartel.co.nz Boost Ltd © 2009

p. 230 http://www.iseatz.com © iSeatz

p. 231 http://www.firehost.com © 2009 FireHost Inc.

p. 231 http://strutta.com Strutta Media, Inc. © 2009

p. 232 http://wpcoder.com WPCoder © 2009

p. 232 http://www.ecolect.net Ecolect, Inc © 2009

p. 232 http://graphik.fi Viljami Salminen © 2009

p. 232 http://www.behance.net Behance, LLC © 2009

p. 233 http://thecssblog.com Ignacio Ricci © 2009

p. 233 **http://www.airbornehealth.com** Airborne © 2010

p. 234 **http://www.actionmethod.com** Behance, LLC © 2009

p. 234 **http://www.holdsworthdesign.com** © 2009 Holds'worth Design

p. 234 **http://www.campaignhq.co.nz** Boost Ltd © 2009

p. 234 **http://www.modalinc.com** Modal, Inc. © 2009

p. 235 **http://www.jayhollywood.com.au** Jay Hollywood © 2010

p. 237 **http://www.bohemiancoding.com** Bohemian Coding © 2009

p. 237 **http://www.blend.uk.com** Blend Creative Ltd. © 2009

p. 237 **http://lamusicblog.com** LA Music Blog, LLC © 2009

p. 237 **http://www.elixirgraphics.com** elixir graphics © 2006-2009

p. 238 **http://www.needanelectrician.co.nz** Adrian Hodge © 2009

p. 238 **http://www.lindtexcellence.com** Lindt & Sprüngli (USA) © 2009

p. 238 **http://www.seydesign.com** seyDoggy © 2010

p. 238 **http://www.nanastreak.com/webdesignersidea/LowertownPrintingCompany** Lowertown Printing Company © 2010

p. 239 **http://www.taoeffect.com** JohnwithanH.com © 2009

p. 239 **http://www.teoskaffa.com** MGB © 2009

p. 240 **http://rockbeatspaper.com** Rockbeatspaper © 2004-2010

p. 241 **http://www.airbnb.com** Airbnb, Inc © 2009

p. 241 **http://www.jointmedias.com** Joint Medias Inc. © 2009

p. 241 **http://fusionwaredesign.com** fusionware design, llc © 2009

p. 242 **http://gandrweb.com/one** GANDR Web © 2010

p. 242 **http://kolor-designs.com/blog** Razvan Horeanga © 2009

p. 242 **http://www.gievesandhawkes.com** gievesandhawkes © 2009

p. 243 **http://www.trippingwords.com** Tripping Words © 2009

p. 243 **http://www.endoscopia.com** American Medical Endoscopy © 2009

p. 243 **http://elliotjaystocks.com** Elliot Jay Stocks © 2009

p. 244 **http://socialsnack.com** Social Snack © 2009

p. 244 **http://www.filesharehq.com** Slipstream Studio © 2009

p. 244 **http://designmess.com** Sean Geng © 2010

p. 245 **http://www.raddsigns.com** RAD designs, LLC © 2009

p. 245 **http://bradcolbow.com** Brad Colbow © 2009

p. 247 **http://www.emotech.com.au** emotech © 2009

p. 247 **http://www.steveprezant.com** Steve Prezant Photography © 2009

p. 247 **http://www.kodu.co.uk** Panduka Senaka © 2009

p. 247 **http://cubicleninjas.com** Cubicle Ninjas, LLC © 2009

p. 248 **http://www.interdevil.com** InterDevil.com (Artur Bobinski) Copyright © 2009. All Rights Reserved.

p. 248 **http://www.falcon-nw.com** FireHost Inc. © 2010

p. 248 **http://pandathemes.com** Panda Themes © 2009

p. 248 **http://www.mindmeister.com** © 2009 MeisterLabs

p. 249 **http://www.blamomedia.ca** blamomedia © 2009

p. 249 **http://www.radiumlabs.com** Radium © 2009

p. 250 **http://www.fmair.com** FM AIR © 2009

p. 250 **http://otrophies.com** SimpleFlame © 2010

p. 250 **http://www.elevationchurch.org** Elevation Church © 2009

p. 250 **http://www.treemolabs.com** Treemo Labs © 2009

p. 251 **http://divita.eu** Philip Seyfi © 2009

p. 251 **http://www.nevilledesign.com** Neville Design Group © 2009

p. 252 **http://www.fhoke.com** FHOKE Limited © 2009

p. 253 **http://www.carsonified.com** Carsonified © 2009

p. 253 **http://www.studioweber.com** StudioWEBER © 2009

p. 253 **http://www.ndesign-studio.com** N.Design Studio © 2009

p. 253 **http://graphik.fi** Viljami Salminen © 2009

p. 253 **http://www.monolinea.com** Kemie Guaida © 2009

p. 254 **http://www.tylergaw.com** Tyler Gaw © 2009

p. 254 **http://www.pixelthread.co.uk** Pixel Thread © 2009

p. 254 **http://www.shayhowe.com** Shay Howe © 2010

p. 254 **http://www.dockerydesign.com** Tyler Dockery © 2009

check out the original
web designer's idea book,
too!

Discover Patrick McNeil's first bestselling desk reference for layout, color and style that web designers have turned to again and again. Based on the author's website, DesignMeltdown.com, you'll find a huge collection of websites organized by a wide variety of criteria. Only the best examples from the website are showcased in this book. You'll see examples of sites before they're redesigned, and also multiple examples of the redesign. You'll find a treasure trove of visual inspiration—helping you see what others have done and how you can adapt those ideas to your own needs.

#Z1756, 256 pages, paperback, ISBN: 978-1-60061-064-6

Also, Visit TheWebDesignersIdeaBook.com

Visit TheWebDesignersIdeaBook.com to learn how to submit your designs for use in future books. Submitting sites is free and open to anyone. You can also sign up for our semi-annual e-mail newsletter to find out about all the opportunities available with this book series.